KV-32

ROPOLI

PRIVATIZATION: IMPLICATIONS FOR CORPORATE CULTURE CHANGE

Cranfield University stands as one of Europe's most specialised advanced teaching and applied research centres in the areas of engineering technology and management. The university itself is unique in that most of its courses are run for postgraduates, and subsequently represents one of the largest centres for applied research in Western Europe.

To my father, Raphael Salama, in memorium

Privatization: Implications for Corporate Culture Change

ALZIRA SALAMA
Cranfield School of Management
Cranfield University

Avebury

Aldershot • Brookfield USA • Hong Kong • Singapore • Sydney

Published by
Avebury
Ashgate Publishing Limited
Gower House
Croft Road
Aldershot
Hants GU11 3HR
England

Ashgate Publishing Company
Old Post Road
Brookfield
Vermont 05036
USA

British Library Cataloguing in Publication Data

Salama, Alzira
Privatization: Implications for Corporate
Culture Change
I. Title
338.925

ISBN 1 85628 912 5

Library of Congress Catalog Card Number: 95-78266

Printed and bound in Great Britain by Ipswich Book Co. Ltd., Ipswich, Suffolk

Contents

Figures and tables

Acknowledgements

Thanks to:

The managers of British Airports Authority, British Airways, British Nuclear Fuels Ltd, Jaguar Cars and Usiminas who provided me with the raw data for this major project.

John Blagden from Cranfield University Press and Sarah Markham from Ashgate Publishing Ltd for their interest in publishing the material which was originally my PhD thesis.

Alex Britnell for her patience, efficiency and restless help in preparing the final document for publication.

Preface

Privatization has become the political creed of the 1990s. Last year alone nationalised firms worth $60 billion (£36 billion) worldwide were privatized. A similar total is forecast for this year, 1995.

Privatization programmes have begun to attract considerable attention from both academics and managers. The literature on privatization is extensive and includes several books. The literature can be categorized as either academic (e.g. the use of economic theories to support the concept of privatization), or political (e.g. arguments which espouse the idea that smaller government is better).

At present the literature lacks a comprehensive, detailed description of the new management approaches necessary for transforming a state owned company into a privately owned one. This book attempts to fill this gap.

In general the change in the ownership of the company leads to a different structure of incentives for management and hence to modifications both in managerial behaviour and company performance. This book explains how managerial behaviour changes as a result of new top management values and beliefs. The company's cultural transformation is analysed.

1 Introduction

This book is addressed to senior management, graduate students and researchers who are involved in the issue of corporate culture change provoked by government deregulation and fiercer market competition. In particular, it can be helpful for those who are involved in the management of change associated with privatization decisions.

Privatization and market deregulation effectively change the business environment and thus increase the demands placed on management in improving long term profitability. Changes in corporate culture are regarded as a prerequisite for redirecting a firm under a transition from the public to the private sector (Hammer et al, 1989).

This book describes the process of modifying historical 'organizational values', and consequently expected managerial behaviour, which Jaguar Cars, British Nuclear Fuels Ltd (BNFL), British Airways (BA), British Airports Authority (BAA) and Usiminas experienced when they were privatized.

This is a research based book which explains in a thorough manner the steps taken by these firms when experiencing fiercer market competition associated with deregulation and privatization decisions. The research on which the findings were based was conducted among firms from different industries in the UK (1987 to 1991) and also in Brazil (1991 to 1992). The common factor that linked them is that they were all undergoing a major process of reshaping their management values and beliefs as a consequence of privatization decisions.

The main conclusion drawn from this study relates to the *process* and the *content/context* of corporate culture change: the *content/context* of corporate culture varies between countries as it reflects nations' different values; it varies between firms as it reflects each organization's industry and history; finally it varies between departments/areas within a firm, as it reflects each department/area's specific sub culture. The *process* of culture change,

1

however, was found to be similar in all five firms under investigation, despite their belonging to different industries and operating in different countries.

One of the learning points which came out of this research is that ownership does not actually trigger culture change. The top management's perceptions of the changes in the business environment are, in fact, the conditions for the process of change which occurred within the firms investigated.

Structure of the book

Chapter Two gives an overview of privatization worldwide; *Chapter Three* explores the impact of privatization on corporate culture change - a model for 'strategic culture change' is provided; *Chapter Four* explains the concept of organization culture from a theoretical viewpoint; *Chapter Five* offers the description and analysis of four British studies; *Chapter Six* discusses the findings of the British case studies - a cross case analysis; *Chapter Seven* describes and analyses the Brazilian case study (Usiminas), *Chapter Eight* discusses the main conclusions and offers a summary of the book, and *Chapter Nine* (Appendices 1, 2 and 3) explains the methodology utilised in the research.

2 Global privatization

Introduction

This chapter offers an overview of the privatization process worldwide. Specific emphasis is given to the privatization programmes in the UK and in Brazil. The role of the Government in the Brazilian and British economies is described in this chapter as a background. The objectives of privatization policies in those two countries are also discussed.

Overview

Since the 1980s privatization has been a major preoccupation of governments of a diversity of political persuasions, and in countries at a wide range of stages of development (Fraser, 1988).

The original term 'privatization' appeared in Britain at the beginning of 1980s as opposed to the term 'nationalisation' of the 1960s to 1970s (Helman, 1991). Privatization is the full or partial transfer of government responsibility to the private sector. It is an attempt to diminish the role of government bureaucracies and enhance the responsibilities of the private and commercial sectors (Utt, 1989). Yarrow (1986) defines privatization as the transfer from the public to the private sector of entitlements to residual profits from operating an enterprise, coupled with any accompanying changes in regulatory policy.

Although the current wave of privatization worldwide was launched in 1979 in the UK, the economic case for privatization is not new. Two centuries ago Adam Smith (1776) argued that:

> In every great monarch in Europe the sale of the Crown lands would produce a very large sum of money which, if applied to the payment of the public debts, would deliver from mortgage a much greater revenue than any which those lands have been afforded

to the Crown ... when the Crown lands had become private property, they would, in the course of a few years, become well improved and well cultivated.

Today, privatization policies are again popular: extensive programmes are under way, not only in mature economies such as the UK, but also in developing countries.

Since 1979, around 7,000 state enterprises have been privatized worldwide. Governments of all political hues, driven by financial expediency more often than ideological conviction, have followed the UK's lead. The idea behind this 'technical' selling, (or changing of ownership) is to increase efficiency. Privatization is not an end in itself, but only a means or a special way to encourage better results in terms of costs, quality and innovation. Worldwide interest in privatization has increased recently for several reasons. These include:

1   The collapse of Communism in the former Soviet Union and its Eastern European allies and the emerging government's determination to transform state owned enterprises into private sector entities.

2   The desire of a growing number of political leaders and their constituents to reduce the size and scope of local and national government.

3   The problem of how governments can continue to provide adequate public services given the reluctance of many citizens to fund regular tax increases.

4   The commitment of some governments to increase public enterprise's efficiency, productivity and responsiveness to customer needs.

5   The desire of many nations to promote free market principles and to establish an enterprise culture.

There is a common motive in many countries to control what have generally been believed to be 'natural monopolies' (i.e. industries in which economies of scale or network economies are so large that it is efficient to have only one producer). Yet private ownership of these industries is the norm in the US. Natural resources and heavy metals industries are frequently nationalised (in Austria, the UK, France, and Norway, for example). Automobiles, steel, tobacco, armaments, banking, oil, aircraft and salt are all industries in which one can find both forms of ownership in Western Europe. In fact, with the exception of the postal service, there is no industry that is exclusively the preserve of the public sector in both Western Europe and the United States.

A worldwide examination of the trend indicates that privatization has just begun. For the 1990s, the greatest challenges lie in Eastern Europe and the USSR. Privatization in these countries is nothing less than a transfer of entire economies from the public sector to the private sector. Privatization developments of fundamental importance also are occurring in other parts of the world. New governments in Mexico, Argentina and Brazil are determined to take vigorous action towards privatization. In addition, the Asian Tigers of the Far East have extensive plans for exposing some of their state industries and utilities to the market disciplines of the private sector.

Privatization is an integral part of the strategic renaissance which is taking place in many Eastern and Western European countries and in countries on other continents as well. It has already had a profound impact on the social, political, macroeconomics and managerial dimensions of governments, government owned enterprises, and newly privatized firms. This impact is certain to increase and become even more widespread as governments further their efforts in this area and as other governments join the privatization movement.

The following two sections focus on the British and the Brazilian privatization programmes.

The British privatization programme

The privatization programme in the UK is the oldest endeavour of its kind in the world. Under the leadership of former Prime Minister, Margaret Thatcher, Britain's Government promised 'to roll back the frontiers of the state'. In 1979 privatization became an important element of the British Government's economic strategy of involving the private sector in activities previously carried out by the public sector in order to reduce the size of the latter.

Background: the role of the state in the British economy

Although some state owned industries had existed in the UK for many years, shortly after World War II ended, the British Government initiated a widespread programme of nationalisation. Founded on the tenets of socialism, nationalisation's goals were to promote greater equality of income, increase the distribution of wealth, and create prosperity throughout the nation. The expected benefits of nationalisation included:

70

1   A decrease in the price of goods and services provided.

2   An increase in the quality of customer service.

3   Higher efficiency and productivity in firms which were nationalised.

It was believed that employees of state owned enterprises would work for the public good and that their decisions and behaviour would reflect what was best for the nation. It was assumed that by appropriating large businesses (many of which were founded by the Victorian entrepreneurs), the state would be able to apply the powers of socialism to redress the abuses which occurred under capitalism. The supporters of nationalisation had such great faith in the enterprises they created that many were given monopoly power. It was thought that the interest of the public was best served by having a single supplier. Competition was considered costly and wasteful to consumers and tax payers.

The post war nationalisation programme proved to be a disappointing failure which severely damaged the British economy. From the mid 1960s through to 1989, for example, nationalised industries' total return on capital invested was always significantly less than the private sector. The industries' total return on capital was close to zero from the early 1970s. Historical comparisons show that the prices of goods and services provided by nationalised industries regularly increased faster than the Retail Price Index. During the years 1970 to 1983, employment costs per employee in the large nationalised industries increased faster than the national average, without equivalent increases in productivity. For example, employment costs per employee in the gas, coal, electricity and telecommunications industries increased 38, 21, 18 and 18 per cent respectively, more than the national average. Contributing to this was the fact that the trade unions, which represented employees in public sector monopolies, were very successful in securing significant pay rises for their members, although worker productivity barely increased. Customer satisfaction with the services and products of nationalised industries was often low, as a survey conducted in 1981 by the National Consumer Council unveiled. The survey found that customers were discontent with rising prices and declining standards and that their expectations were not being met.

Whatever the causes of poor performance in the nationalised industries, the long term results of the nationalisation programmes in the UK are quite clear: lack of competition in important segments of the economy, limited choices for consumers, higher prices for goods and services sold by nationalised firms (which fuelled inflation nationwide), customer dissatisfaction, low employee morale and productivity, political manoeuvring, management indecision and economic stagnation. To deal with the poor performance of nationalised industries both the Labour and Conservative parties have, over the years, imposed standards and controls to provide an environment similar to a free market. Although those attempts sometimes were successful, they did not yield long term solutions. Attempting to control the industries' behaviour by improving surrogate market forces simply does not deal with the fundamental problem of state ownership.

The privatization programme which was initiated by the Thatcher Government was a direct strategy to deal with the poor performance of the nationalised firms and with the social, political, macroeconomic, and managerial problems associated with them. For the Thatcher Government privatization involved more that the transfer of state owned businesses to the private sector. It was part of an overall plan to create a truly free market economy in the UK. Special arrangements are made to encourage employees to become shareholders when a majority of the shares in the firm they work for are sold by a public flotation on the stock exchange.

The Government of the UK has spent more than a dozen years privatizing nationalised industries valued at over £29 billion. The process itself is intricate and lengthy, taking up to several years to complete. Its objectives include not only selling state owned business, but increasing each business efficiency through competition, encouraging more equal distribution of wealth, and strengthening the UK's economy and its position in international markets. The process has been used to privatize different size businesses from diverse industries.

The British experience with privatization seems to show that exposing industries to the financial disciplines of the market place generally creates better managed companies that produce higher quality goods and services and provide enhanced value to their customers.

Objectives of privatization in the UK

1   Improving efficiency by increasing competition and allowing firms to borrow from the capital market.

2   Reducing the public sector borrowing requirement.

3   Easing problems of public sector pay determination.

4   Reducing government involvement in enterprise decision making.

5   Widening the ownership of economic assets.

6   Encouraging employee ownership of shares in their companies.

7   Redistributing income and wealth.

Prior to German reunification, the UK had the most rapid and extensive programme of privatization in Western Europe.

The Brazilian privatization programme

In the newly developing democracies of Latin America, the rapid pace of privatization and political stabilisation has been astonishing (Sears, 1992). By Citibank's calculations, there have been more than 150 privatizations completed over the last three years with Argentina, Brazil, Chile, Mexico and Venezuela. Revenues from these privatizations are estimated at over $50 billion (£30 billion).

Latin America, home of stability, democracy, low inflation, and economic growth, wishes it to be known that it has no connection to the other Latin America plagued by out of control inflation, debt crises, and military dictatorships. Many of the countries have demonstrated the ability to stick to viable economic reform programmes to attract capital from residents and non residents, achieve growth, and return to the international markets. The greatest beneficiaries of privatization in Latin America have been multinational corporations and large domestic conglomerates, which have taken the opportunity to consolidate their oligopolistic control of some of the most dynamic sectors of the economy (Rhodes, 1992).

Brazil is the tenth largest economy in the world, four places behind Great Britain and ahead of all developing countries such as Mexico, South Korea and Taiwan. It is by far the largest economy in Latin America.

Brazil, with its population of 155 million and gross domestic product of $450 billion (£273 billion) is Latin America's largest economy, and remains one of the most attractive Latin American markets for US business. Brazil is undergoing a number of dramatic economic reforms that are positioning the country to resume economic growth and development in the medium to long term. Trade liberalisation, privatization, deregulation, fiscal austerity, and tax reform are the keys for the new economic reform programme in that country.

Table 1
GDP - Brazil versus other Latin American countries (1993)

		Nominal GDP (US$bn)
1	Brazil	456.0
2	Mexico	360.4
3	Argentina	255.3
4	Venezuela	59.2
5	Chile	43.7
6	Colombia	*43.5
7	Peru	*13.1
8	Uruguay	*41.1
9	Ecuador	*14.3
10	Dominican Republic	9.5
11	Costa Rica	8.0
12	Bolivia	*6.6
13	Panama	*6.6
14	Paraguay	*6.4

* 1992   Source: Consensus Economics Inc

Background: The role of the state in the Brazilian economy The Brazilian economy's development, as well as other countries of late industrialisation, grew out of a peculiar symbiosis among the public sector, private capital and foreign capital.   Three basic economic sectors, steel, oil and electricity, constituted the nucleus of the state's segment of the economy.

In Brazil, the state's presence has been strong as ever since the country became a republic. The idea that the state should carry out the main task of overcoming the barriers to capitalism development dates back to the 1930s. But only in the 1940s did the state begin to take effective action in the productive sector. The magnitude of the state's intervention in the Brazilian economy in the last decades is undeniable, in terms of both the weight of the state's productive sector and the state's enormous capacity to control the funds directed to finance the development process.

After 1950, the state adopted the policy of consciously intervening in the industrialisation process. The oil monopoly was proclaimed in 1953 with the creation of Petrobras. Brazilian industrialisation underwent decisive structural changes during 1956 to 1960. It represented an intensive industrialisation effort over a short period of time. It was at this time that the state productive sector began to grow with the simultaneous materialisation of several large projects.

In the political sphere, an authoritarian state was established in 1964, increasing the public sector's potential in detriment of the private sector. In 1967 the Government sought to organise state activity by means of an

9

Administrative Reform, which created separate entities and procedures for the direct and indirect administration. From 1968 to 1973, the rate of economic growth rose very quickly, characterising the period known as the 'Brazilian Miracle'. The 'Brazilian Miracle' period was marked by the establishment of a significant number of state companies, diversification movement by means of establishing subsidiary companies. Another fifteen federal government companies and forty nine state government companies were born between 1960 and 1969. This trend became even stronger from 1970 to 1976, when seventy new federal government companies and sixty new state government companies were created.

The state productive sector thus underwent substantial horizontal and vertical growth and began to engage itself directly in several private sector's business segments. It not only competed with the private sector but also took the space which should normally be occupied by private enterprise. The 1980s saw the end of economic growth with a return to the indebtedness model adopted during the 1970s. A period of economic stagnation began, accompanied by a strong drop in investment rate. At the same time, chronic and resistant inflation took over.

The scenario encountered by the Collor de Mello Administration, in March 1990, was marked by economic stagnation with spiralling inflation and strong deterioration of public finances. Prepared for challenges, the new government surprised the nation with an unprecedented economic stabilisation plan consisting of extremely strict and far reaching measures designed to deal directly with the problems of the Brazilian economy.

The Collor Administration was committed to turning Brazil into a free market economy and removing heavy state controls imposed by the military. Import tariffs were reduced significantly and an ambitious privatization programme undertaken. International investors and bankers viewed the opening of the economy positively. Still in 1991, the Government eliminated price controls and gave the economy total freedom to establish its prices.

Announced as one of the objectives of the economic reforms launched in March 1990, the Brazilian privatization programme took a total of seventeen months to be started in October 1991, when the common shares of Usiminas were sold at an auction. The long period that elapsed between the announcement of the programme and its actual implementation basically reflects the natural precautions required of the organisers of a programme of such a kind. From October 1991 to November 1994, twenty four companies were privatized, including the following sectors: petrochemicals, 9; metallurgy, 8; fertilizers, 4; transportation material, 1; aircraft engine overhaul, 1; and shipping, 1.

In addition to the general objective of redefining the role of the state, the Brazilian privatization programme aims at the following goals:

* long term fiscal adjustment, reduction of public deficit and of the necessity for restructuring and financing of assets and liabilities of the public sector.

* state reform, redefinition of the role of the state in the Brazilian economy and concentration of state resources and efforts in social areas such as education, health, housing, security, sanitation and others.

* transfer to the private sector of all activities considered under the previous development model as strategic for the industrialisation process.

* reduction of public domestic and foreign debt.

* stimulate modernisation of the domestic industry thorough increased competition.

* strengthening of the capital market to promote wider share ownership.

An important characteristic of the Brazilian privatization programme, that should be kept in mind for comparison purposes with similar experiences in other Latin American countries, is its concentration on companies of the manufacturing sector, not including companies from the financial and public service sector, as is the case in Mexico and Argentina.

3 Privatization: Implications for corporate culture change

Introduction

This chapter discusses the impact of privatization on organizational culture. It highlights the new behaviour required by people within organizations in order to survive in a private sector business environment. The changes required from management are discussed. A specific and fundamental section is devoted to the process of implementing culture change within firms. An integrative model of strategic culture change, which resulted from data collected in the UK (from Jaguar, BNFL, BA and BAA) and in Brazil (from a large steel organization, Usiminas), is presented and discussed. Grounds for generalisation are presented.

Privatization: implications for management

The reduction of direct government ownership and regulation enables firms to reveal their talent and potential, following the belief that the role of the 'market' is an important factor in incentives and motivation (Muti, 1990). However, improved performance is not an automatic effect of privatization and the acquisition of the required skills should be facilitated within the privatization process.

The introduction of entrepreneurial behaviour is required to provide ex-state enterprises with the dynamism needed for the expected transformation in the firm's efficiency.

The selling of shares in state owned industries cannot create new powerful management, nor can it guarantee a company's survival.

When privatized, a company is forced by external influences to re-think its future. A management with long term vision will anticipate this change (whilst still state owned) and prepare strategies for managing it and ensuring the success of the privatization. In developing these strategies the management must address the issue of entrepreneurial vision. For that, changes in the employee's working related values are necessary. A transformation in the organization culture is then required before a new global organizational strategy can be formulated.

How do companies change from being bureaucratic and conservative to being innovative and entrepreneurial? An emphasis on cost cutting, innovation, commercial awareness and adaptability to the market has been encouraged. These changes have fed through into the role of line managers, who are seen as one of the main agents of change. They have become what the 'delivery mechanism' for the new culture, for example through their enhanced role in employee communications, as well as 'designers and drivers of change'.

Managers are encouraged to be on the look out for 'new growth opportunities'. Entrepreneurship has been encouraged, especially where companies are trying to diversify into new markets. Management control systems have been reformed to devolve much greater authority to the line. Operational managers were expected to develop a 'business orientation' rather than concern themselves primarily with the technicalities of production management. Considerable delegation of authority has also taken place in the areas of personnel and industrial relations.

Private sector structures are argued to be more effective in both the motivation and control of managers. State sector salaries are usually unrelated to the financial performance of the firm. In contrast, remuneration packages in the private sector tend to link financial rewards to the performance of the firm.

A competitive environment fosters efficiency since failure to compete reduces market share and profits. The firm is under continuous pressure to pay attention to costs and to the requirements of its customers. It is driven to innovate in order to fund different products and to lower costs.

As Crockford (1994) points out, the justification for privatization is based on the belief that private sector organizations are necessarily better at managing business than the public sector. However, much attention and consideration must be given to how these managers and organizations can acquire the necessary skills for success in a private sector environment. This book will tackle this issue specifically.

Privatization is most effective if a change of ownership is combined with measures to strengthen competition (Parker, 1995). But for both, for changes in ownership and in the competitive environment to occur, and for the firm to function effectively in such circumstances, the firm must possess particular management characteristics: appropriate skills are necessary to managing in a market economy - a culture change is required.

14

The individual self actualisation, and the employees' individual participation have now become more important than the 'social or collective' needs in a government owned bureaucracy. How to achieve the required transformation in management has been the crucial challenge for recently privatized companies. Redesigning systems and introducing new methods and procedures, at first glance, represent the easiest way to achieve that. However, the findings of this study reveal that unless people change their working related values first, new methods are deemed to fail. It is necessary to challenge people's ways of thinking prior to the introduction of new working methods. The next section is devoted to this particular issue, i.e it describes the steps utilised by Jaguar, BNFL, BA, BAA and Usiminas in their efforts to modify people's attitudes and behaviour.

Strategic culture change implementation: a universal approach

The main conclusion drawn from the five case studies, four in the UK (Jaguar, BNFL, BA and BAA) and one in Brazil (Usiminas), was that although the contents of culture vary between companies and countries, the *process of change* is similar. This means that the *steps* companies pursue in their battle for transforming their well established culture are actually the same in all five firms investigated. The success of the change process relies on *how* each company accomplished each of these six steps. This is explained in Chapters 5, 6 and 7.

The integrative model of culture change

A model is a very simplistic way to describe the reality. However, this model has been useful to convey the results of this research in terms of how to implement a strategy for corporate culture change triggered by a discontinuity in the business environment in which firms operate. This model has also been useful as a basis for discussion in the MBA and general management short courses at Cranfield School of Management. It gives the managers an overview of the process and also how the different steps integrate with each other.

This model encapsulates primarily my learning from the major research conducted in four firms in the UK experiencing major changes provoked by market deregulation and privatization. Furthermore, this model has been tested in a major Nipo Brazilian steel organization which was the first organization to become private during the Denationalisation Programme of President Collor in 1990 in Brazil.

The model describes the six specific steps which resulted from the analysis of implementation of culture change in five firms under investigation. These steps are not purported to be comprehensive, but instead indicate some of the common managerial actions utilised by firms which proved essential for a smooth transition process.

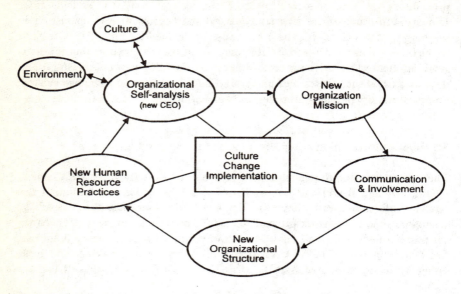

Figure 1 The integrative model of culture change

Vital to understand the above model are the following dimensions:

1   Integration

No step in isolation, no matter how perfectly it is implemented, will contribute for the success of the transition from culture A (historical) to culture B (desired). An integration of all six stages of the process is fundamental for the achievement of the change process's goals.

2   Culture evolution versus culture reconstruction

Empirical evidence (UK and Brazil) shows that when dealing with change processes, one might prefer to think in an evolutionary way. It means the historical culture needs to be understood, challenged and improved, not destroyed. This approach helps to prevent/minimise possible resistance

16

coming from those who have been contributing to the firm for a long period of time.

Description and explanation of the six steps compounding the corporate culture change process.

Step 1 Organization self analysis: culture-environment fit

Corporate culture is created by founders/top leaders to help organizations in their survival and growth process within a certain business environment. This culture is built around a central set of values that pervade every aspect of companies' operations. Employees are indoctrinated to internalise these values, and those who do not rarely last. These values are the lifeblood of the firm, creating the standards and providing the direction for growth and development.

To ensure an appropriate fit (culture-environment) a regular/constant assessment of this relationship is necessary as the business' environment changes quite rapidly. Therefore, to maintain an appropriate culture, top leaders would initiate an analysis of the mentioned fit on a regular basis. The analysis of the culture-environment fit is the fundamental step to prevent any problems of mismatching between the way people think and behave within the organization and the required way of thinking and behaving dictated by the competitive global business.

When a gap is found in the culture-environment fit there is a need for implementing a culture change strategy. This gap often occurs as a consequence of a long period of organizational inertia, i.e. lack of technical and/or management innovations. This inertia leads firms to bad financial situations, sometimes a crisis is established. The size of the gap will dictate whether it will be a major intervention or a subtle one.

The outcome of Step 1 will be the answer to the following question: which working related values are necessary to be kept, and which ones are necessary to be modified? This is then the starting point of the change process: the awareness of each company's weakness and strength in cultural terms. A development in culture is then initiated once the level of awareness is achieved.

Step 2 New core mission (what we stand for)

Often, when a gap in culture-environment fit is found (Step 1), a need for rethinking a new core mission is perceived. The new mission is established and then communicated across the organization.

Step 3 Communication

All available means of communicating the new core mission are then utilised to convey, in a positive way, the new direction of the firm and the reasons for that; information on the culture-environment fit analysis is given, this include the awareness of the strength and weakness of the historical culture as well as the direction necessary for organizational survival and growth.

Step 4 Involvement

Seminars, training activities, workshops are utilised to foster active participation on how to go from culture A to culture B. Different views coming from groups are analysed. Following the organization structure, this movement is more effective if initiated by top levels, cascading down to shop floor levels. Commitment must come from top management if we expect a smooth process of change. Imposing new ways of behaviour is certainly the easiest path to bring about resistance. Involvement is vital.

Step 5 New criteria for recruitment/selection, new training and development programmes, new reward/appraisal systems

As a new core mission is developed, the way to get there requires a different frame of mind. Leaders are now challenged to review their own behaviour and values. Training and development are useful tools in this direction. New criteria to recruit, select and promote leaders must be established. Appraisal and reward systems are redesigned to reinforce different behaviour. A new culture starts to emerge gradually in the organization. The new human resource system will be reinforcing the required managerial behaviour (see figure 2).

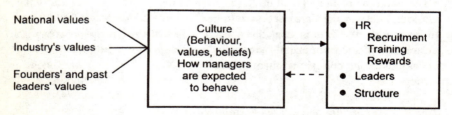

Figure 2 How culture is created and maintained

Changes in organizational structure can facilitate cultural and behavioural transformations within organizations (Ivancevich and Donnelly, 1975).

Porter and Lawler (1965) suggested that a flat structure was not superior to a tall one. Nevertheless, a flat structure was better for fulfilling autonomy and self actualisation needs. A proliferation of hierarchical levels of management encourages centralisation of authority and job specialisation (Chandler, 1962). These structural characteristics lead to a low level of job autonomy with suppression of personal judgement and initiative and failure to develop managerial talent. Redesigning the organization structure will facilitate the emergence of a different relationship between people and areas within organization. For example, a flat organization design, together with other tools (e.g. training) can facilitate a closer relationship between supervisor/employee. A matrix organization design can facilitate the emergence of a flexible workforce behaviour. However, there is no better way to organise the work. The organizational structure is usually revised by top management according to the specific needs to be achieved, the new mission.

The role of managers during the culture change implementation process

As explained through the six steps, implementing a culture change model strategy is a lengthy and demanding process, especially when the firm has been static for a long period of time. Senior management must take the lead in setting new organizational goals, opening communication, accepting failure, empowering middle management, and creating an environment in which new ideas are welcomed. Middle managers are the catalysts in terms of 'overcoming' the natural barriers, implementing new structures and systems, and lessening bureaucracy.

Discontinuity in the business environment gives rise to internal turbulence. The extent to which this internal adjustment is achieved through a kind of 'controlled chaos' built around innovativeness, risk taking and proactiveness will define the successful privatization process.

The strategic model for culture change described in this section highlights the six steps that seem to be essential for a successful culture change process. However, the model alone does not allow the reader to understand the 'ins and outs' of each step, the problems CEO encountered when implementing the culture change strategies and the ways they found to overcome their difficulties. This is explained in detail in the case studies (see Chapters 5, 6 and 7).

The case studies explain how each company went through these six steps. The description and analysis step by step of the transformation of an 'old culture' into a 'new culture' is rich in itself. Such analysis leads the reader to feel the process and to experience some of the fears, resistance and difficulties which characterise the implementation process.

4 Theoretical views on culture and culture change

Introduction

This chapter provides an overview of the literature on culture per se, on corporate culture and on corporate culture change. The important lesson that I have learned through this research is that to change people's behaviour, it is fundamental to deal with people's ways of thinking first, their ideas and values. This chapter aims to explain how different groups of people think differently, and why.

What is culture? (its origins in anthropological literature)

E.B. Tylor, in 1871, was probably the first to use the word 'culture' in English (Laraia, 1986; Kroeber and Kluckhohn, 1952; Hofstede, Newjen, Ohayv and Sanders, 1990). He emphasised the human being's capacity to learn and transfer his knowledge to others. Unlike the biological attributes of mankind, culture is the result of a learning process instead of a genetic human characteristic. The ideas of continuity, creation, accumulation and transmission of culture independent of biological heredity were the key issues for Tylor (Kroeber and Parsons, 1958).

The anthropologists, Kroeber and Kluckhohn (1952), consider that, although some aspects of culture are nearly universal (such as child care), groups differ culturally according to their specific history and learning experiences. For example, different cultures, such as USA and Japan, place different emphasis on time (Hick & Gullet, 1981).

In summary, culture means all forms of collectively learned human behaviour. It varies from group to group. For instance, what is accepted within one group can be considered absurd within another group. Hence, culture influences what behaviour is approved or disapproved. This is illustrated by Laraia (1986):

> Culture is a great source of security that tells us frequently what is right or wrong (p. 15).

Sathe (1985) considers that two major schools of cultural anthropology have influenced the current concept of culture: the adaptionists and the ideationists. The first is based on what is directly observable about the members of a community (speech, language, dress). The later school prefers to look at what is shared in the community members' minds (aspirations, values, beliefs and other ideas people have in common). This research investigates corporate culture under these two perspectives, i.e. analysing both the directly observable and the values, beliefs and assumptions of the members of an organization.

The concept of culture is usually reserved for societies, or is applied equally to other human collectivities or categories: organizations, professions, religions, or families. In a very simple and general way, the current use of the term 'culture' refers to the specific way of life of a group of people.

Culture and social systems

Kroeber and Parsons (1958) tried to explain the 'confusion' among the concepts of culture and of social system. According to them, for a considerable period, there was a condensed concept of culture and society. This condensed concept was perhaps a consequence of Durkheim (1953) speaking of society as meaning essentially the same thing as Tylor (1871) meant by culture. Nowadays, however, it is believed that further distinctions need to be made in the use of these two concepts: culture and social systems. The following paragraphs explain these differences.

Kroeber and Parsons (1958), refer to culture as transmitted and created content and patterns of values, ideas, and other symbolic meaningful systems as factors in the shaping of human behaviour and of the artifacts produced through behaviour. They suggest that the term social system be used to designate the specifically relational system of interaction among individuals.

From all this I concluded that the distinction between culture and social system is a matter of levels of understanding. Systems of social interaction can be superficially observed and also described. However, they are rooted in culture, i.e. rooted in the transmitted and created patterns of values and ideas (see figure 3). The image of an iceberg may represent our way of seeing them.

As with an iceberg, in order to effectively deal with the social system, it is necessary, first, to deal with culture.

Social System (Visible part of the iceberg, easy to observe)

*Culture (Hidden part of the iceberg, **stronger** but invisible)*

Figure 3 Culture and social system (two parts of the same dimension)

What is corporate culture?

This section is devoted mainly to the different views and concepts of corporate culture rather than to its methodological aspect. The latter is analysed in the appendix.

The idea of corporate culture, since the early 1980s, has acquired the status of a dominant concept in the popular and academic management literature of the US and UK. A recent search of an 'online' data base, ABI Inform, shows that in the last five years approximately 1,800 articles dealt with corporate culture. Of all these, less than two per cent were concerned with the links between corporate culture and human resources management. More specifically, the subject of corporate culture has been dealt with in special issues of American journals such as *Organizational Dynamics* (1983) and *Administrative Science Quarterly* (1983). The English *Journal of Management Studies* (1986) devoted one issue exclusively to studies on corporate culture.

Some controversial views on the idea of corporate culture are quite radical, for instance, while some scholars agree that 'organizational culture merits a discipline in management studies' (Hofstede, 1986), other authors deny not merely the importance of culture in organizations, but even its existence:

> Culture is a word that is common enough, just a touch high falutin, and perfect for the kind of oversimplification that television and video cassette requires. The serious business manager, however, will lose nothing by ignoring it... his brain may be clearer if he expunges the term from his consciousness altogether (Thackray, 1986, p. 69).

This confusion surrounding the concept of corporate culture is related to both its definition and the methods of investigating it. For example, while there are multiple definitions, they tend to be vague and overly general. This situation stems from the many disciplines interested in this topic, which increases richness, but does not necessarily increase clarity. Anthropologists, sociologists, psychologists and others bring with them their particular paradigms and research methodologies. This creates difficulties in reaching consensus on construct definitions as well as on making them operational.

Much attention has been paid to either simple descriptions of corporate culture, ignoring its ambiguities (see Watson, 1963; Harrison, 1987), or to exploring ways of manipulating it; or to changing and reshaping cultures [see Kilmann et al (1986); Lorsch (1986); Meares (1986); Meyerson & Martin (1987) and Edwards & Kleiner (1988)]. This present review, however, aims first to devote some time to clarifying this complex concept, secondly to explore the mechanisms that create and maintain corporate culture and thirdly to explore the idea of 'culture change'.

Concepts of corporate culture

The concept of corporate culture has been widely utilised by organizational theorists and researchers to explain mainly those patterns of behaviour which differentiate one organization from another. The emphasis has been mainly on showing how each organization is unique.

Nevertheless, some authors, 'the typologists', tend to use the concept of corporate culture to classify the similarities among organizations. For example, Harrison (1987) classified organizations into four different groups: the power culture, the role culture, the achievement culture and the support culture. Although he has explained how each of these types of culture functions, he fails to link them to each organization's history. Therefore, Harrison's approach to culture seems to be static (based on 'real time' data analysis), rather than a 'processual' one (based on both historical and real time data analysis). Through avoiding historical analysis, his study lacks information about how these types of culture were created and developed.

Definitions of corporate culture vary from author to author in the available management literature. Nevertheless, some common definitions are shown in table 2.

Jacques (1951) was perhaps the first to use the concept of culture for studying organizations. He speaks of the superficial level of culture - the way of doing things - and relates this to the history of an organization.

Van Mannen's (1977) definition of corporate culture emphasises its role in the socialisation process, especially of newcomers. Harrison (1987) refers to culture as a combination of the social norms, values and preoccupations of an organization. Deal and Kennedy (1982) refer to culture also as social norms, but they emphasise the power of those norms or rules as a managerial control system. Pascale and Athos (1981), in turn, see culture as a philosophy concerned mainly with human resources and marketing issues.

Both Sathe's (1985) and Schein's (1985a) definitions of corporate culture refer to a hidden part of the iceberg (see figure 3). They both consider culture as a set of 'assumptions', often unstated and pre conscious. For them, in order to decipher these assumptions it is not enough to carry on observations, (a technique used by ethnomethodologists): probing interviews are necessary in order to uncover the assumptions and taken for granted values, i.e. how people think instead of just what people do. This is the approach adopted by the present research.

Table 2
Definitions of corporate culture

Jacques 1951	'The culture of the factory is its customary and traditional way of thinking and doing of things, which is shared to a greater or lesser degree by all its members, and which new members must learn, and at last partially accept, in order to be accepted into service in the firm.' (p. 251)
Van Maanen 1977	'The rules of the game for getting along in the organisation, the ropes that a newcomer must learn in order to become an accepted member.' (p.35)
Pascale and Athos 1981	'The philosophy that guides an organization's policy towards employees and/or customers.' (p.43)
Deal and Kennedy 1982	'Corporate culture is defined as a system of formal and informal rules, that spell out how people ought to behave most of the time.' (p. 78)
Schein 1985	'A pattern of basic assumptions developed by a given group as it learns to cope with its problems of external adaptation and internal integration.' (p.28)
Sathe 1985	'The set of important assumptions (often unstated) that members of a community share in common.' (p. 44)
Harrison 1987	'A combination of values, preoccupations, social structure, norms and mores.' (p. 11)

How corporate culture differs from one organization to another

Morgan (1988) stated that we now live in an 'organizational society'; organizations share many common attributes and influence most of our waking hours in a similar way. However, studies of corporate culture do not focus primarily on those attributes of culture which are similar among organizations. They concentrate on understanding those which distinguish one organization from another.

To understand culture and 'grasp it' requires an integrative 'mind set'; this differs from that required for dealing with other organizational issues such as profits and amount of sales. Culture seems to result from a combination of interlinked elements. These are discussed below.

The influence of national values influence on corporate culture McClelland (1961) in his studies suggested that attitudes toward achievement and work vary quite widely from society to society. For example, according to him, society influences organizations and people through the educational system and other social institutions. If we believe that McClelland is right, we consequently believe that national values affect organizational culture. According to Adler (1983), people in organizations reveal previous conditioning by society and many instilled attitudes and beliefs - a prior culture already in place.

Although it has been argued by different theorists [see, for example, Adler and Jelinek (1986); Hofstede (1980)], that the impact of national culture on the behaviour of people within organizations is very significant, this is not within the scope of the present study. It focuses on those cultural characteristics which make an organization unique. Besides, it studies the way in which those cultural characteristics impinge on people's behaviour and how this changes in response to environmental constraints.

The influence of the industry dominating values on corporate culture The literature reveals that different industries reveal distinctive norms and values. As pointed out by Gordon (1985), different industries have developed different cultural patterns to suit their business demands. Thackray (1986) considers that to gain credibility, the corporate culture movement must somehow build bridges between the culture of society and that of the industry. Thackray considers that there are some industries where there is little variety in corporate culture; oil and gas, for instance, or steel and chemicals. In other industries there might be more latitude for firms to evolve distinctively: retailing, fast foods and air transport, for instance. The culture of a small business and a conglomerate must have obvious differences. These dominant values in an industry affect norms about secrecy, political actions, dress and acceptable moral behaviour (Thackray, 1986). This author emphasises the influence of industry dominating characteristics and of national values in the process of creating organizational culture. His approach is limited because it neglects the values of founders and leaders in shaping culture.

The influence of founders' and past leaders' values on corporate culture The strong links that exist between corporate culture and founders' and past leaders' values have been highlighted by different organizational theorists, in particular, by Schein (1983a, 1985a). Based on his consultancy experience and action research, he concluded that leaders create and manage corporate cultures. As he states:

> Founders put their imprint on the culture by bringing in people who share certain beliefs and values with the founder and those people will eventually share them with others as they identify increasingly with the founder and the enterprise (Schein, 1983a, p. 18).

Schein (1985b) highlights the process of learning culture. He says that people in organizations repeat what works and give up what does not. He argues:

> For example, if a company is created with its founder's belief that the way to succeed is either to provide good service to customers or to treat employees as the organization's major resource or always to sell the lowest priced product in the market place, and if action based on that belief succeeds in the market place, then the group will learn to repeat whatever worked and gradually to accept this as a shared view of how the world really is, thereby creating its own culture (p. 32).

Gordon (1985) also reinforces the influence of leaders' values in creating culture. He considers that if a CEO is strongly committed to the concept that profitability is driven primarily by cost control and is further committed to stability and growth of quarterly earnings, it is unlikely that a single unit, department or division will develop a culture that values programmes that are innovative, long term, expansive, and risky.

In order to sum up the important elements which seem to be responsible for the creation of culture in organizations, a framework is appropriate, (see figure 4). Contrary to many introspective approaches on corporate culture (see Schein, 1983a, and his emphasis on leader's values), this framework reveals a wider perspective. Besides the influence of top leaders' values on creating corporate culture, it also considers the dominating values of the industry and of the nation in this process.

Although I have acknowledged the influence of national values on corporate culture, this present study does not aim to show these links. Rather, it explores the founder's and leaders' values and those of the industry in the process of creating and transforming corporate culture. This study focuses only on British industries. This approach was chosen in order to limit the scope of the research topic.

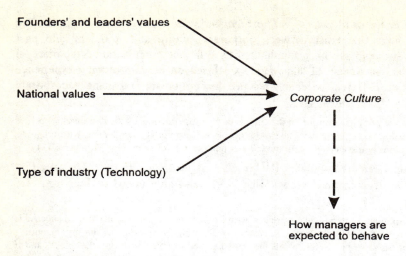

Founders' and leaders' values

National values

Type of industry (Technology)

Corporate Culture

How managers are
expected to behave

Figure 4 How corporate culture forms

What is culture change?

This book analyses one aspect of the process of change within organizations, namely culture change, and its impact upon managerial careers.

Deal and Kennedy (1982, p. 15) consider that 'any organizational change is a culture change' and that any modification occurring in the way firms operate will always require new work related values. Thus, for them, organizational change is synonymous with culture change. Similarly, other authors, such as Morgan and Smircich (1980) and Burrell and Morgan (1982) tend to study organizations as cultures. Conceptually, I agree with these theorists, but from an empirical perspective, if I adopted their approach, it would be more complex to identify the research problem. Therefore, for this reason, I have preferred to use Tichy's (1982) classification of strategic management change on which to base this research topic.

According to Tichy (1982), strategic organizational changes are divided into three distinct areas as shown in figure 5.

Table 3
Strategic organizational changes

The technical area:	The way in which work is organized and products are sold. It involves assessing the environment, aligning structure to strategy and fitting people to roles.
The political area:	Distribution of power, balancing power across groups and managing successful policies.
The cultural area:	Selection of 'adequate' people to build or reinforce culture, development to mould organizational culture and arrangement of rewards to shape culture.

As Tichy (1982) suggests, an effective organizational strategic change should ideally include an alignment of all three areas. However, to understand the process of change, it is necessary to concentrate upon the individual strands as shown in figure 5.

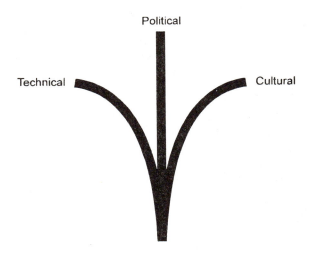

Figure 5 Strands of strategic change

This study is limited to looking at the last aspect of strategic organizational change, as classified by Tichy, namely culture change. The investigation of culture change, in this book, basically involves the analysis of how the organization goes through the process of modifying some of its values, beliefs and assumptions and ultimately altering the way managers are expected to

29

behave.   To understand culture change, though, it was first necessary to understand the way culture was formed in these four organizations. Furthermore, how this change process impinges upon managerial career systems, i.e. on the ways in which a company selects, promotes, develops and rewards its managers was explored.

5 The British case studies

Introduction

This chapter examines the impact of culture change upon four UK organizations when experiencing 'major changes' associated with the process of privatization. These companies are: Jaguar Cars, British Nuclear Fuels Limited (BNFL), British Airways (BA) and British Airports Authority (BAA).

Immediately after its election (May 1979), the new Conservative Government, led by Mrs Margaret Thatcher as Prime Minister, initiated a radical programme of deregulation and privatization of industry and services in the UK. Walters (1990) considers that there is much more to 'going private' than merely transferring ownership from the state to private investors. Walters suggests that profound modifications are necessary in the culture of nationalised organizations if they are to succeed as privatized companies.

The following four case studies explain the process of transition that these four British firms experienced.

Jaguar Cars case study

Introduction

Jaguar was the first company (the pilot) to be studied in this major research. The pilot study was extremely important to test the method I had chosen to investigate the problem at hand. Some weaknesses, however, were found when the first draft of the data analysis was produced. Based on the lessons learnt in this pilot study, there was an attempt to improve both the collection and the analysis of the data in the following case studies.

In addition, the Jaguar case study is described in a different format from the others. It is presented as a self contained paper, i.e. some theoretical concepts are discussed in addition to the empirical data as found in the others. The reason for this emphasis on theory is that I found it necessary, in the early stage of the research, to match the findings with the literature in order to understand in a 'holistic' way the issue I was investigating. So, although the theoretical part may reiterate some of the issues discussed in Chapter 4, it illustrates how I saw the problem under study at the beginning of the research project. The evolution of my ideas is noticeable in the course of the next case studies.

The problem

It is claimed by the UK Government that privatization increases efficiency by provoking organizational change and emphasizing a more entrepreneurial style of management. Organizational change implies, mainly, re-assessment of the company's values and beliefs (David, 1984), in that it must imply a culture change. It was argued by the top management in Jaguar, that the existing corporate culture was inappropriate for the company's survival, considering the new environmental constraints.

A briefing on the company

Jaguar is engaged in the design, development and sale of luxury motor cars. It was a public company until 1984. During the period under investigation (August 1988), Jaguar was employing 12,500 people and producing more than 50,000 cars per year. The United States was its major market followed, in order of importance, by the United Kingdom and Germany. In 1984, the firm became privatized in line with the UK current Government policies. In 1988 Jaguar faced an increasingly competitive global environment and its problems were compounded by the fluctuations in the exchange rates (US dollars - Sterling). Since the privatization, the Government held forty per cent of the company shares. In 1991, however, this 'golden' share would have expired and the company would no longer be protected from takeover.[1]

Definition of terms

The prevailing corporate culture in this case study refers to the values and assumptions shared by most members of an organization as a result of the history and the previous learning experience. They are the 'rules of the game', which spell out how people should behave most of the time in order to be accepted in the social environment of today. Prevailing culture is made explicit by the formal and informal procedures held by a particular organization (Deal and Kennedy, 1982).

The perceived appropriate corporate culture, in turn, refers to the new set of values and assumptions considered by the management to be relevant in order for the organization to become more profitable and able to succeed in the changeable and competitive commercial environment. It implies a futurist perspective. Hence, these values and beliefs represent the 'rules of the game', which spell out how people should behave most of the time in order to be accepted in the social environment of tomorrow.

Managerial careers refers to the criteria used by the organization both to select and to promote managers. It focuses upon the analysis of which managerial profile the organization searches for when it selects executives, and which managerial profile the organization reinforces when it rewards executives by using the promotion system - upgrading them in the career ladder. In addition, it looks at the way the selected organizations plan programmes for developing their managers in order to better prepare them for the organization's needs.

Background/history

Data relating to Jaguar's history was fundamental to a better understanding of the prevailing culture. The data was gathered from Porter (1988) and also through interviews.

In 1922 Sir William Lyons established the company. In 1935 Jaguar was floated as a public firm. During the late 1950s and the early 1960s, a lot of smaller independent companies emerged. Intensive internal competition took place in the UK in the 1960s, all companies, including Jaguar, were struggling

33

and many failed. Hence, in the mid 1960s Jaguar was merged with other companies and the Government took over. Production levels rose between 1970 and 1974 despite considerable management and structural changes taking place at this time, e.g. the retirement of Sir William Lyons in 1972 and the progressive merger of the Jaguar business with the other automotive interests of British Leyland Motor Company (BLMC).

In 1979 there were manufacturing problems. Production fell due to serious difficulties with the quality and reliability of the cars. The continuation of the production shortfall into 1980, together with a poor United Kingdom sales performance, adverse exchange rates and a strike over job grading, gave rise to substantial losses. From 1972 to 1980 Jaguar was managed by a succession of different people and almost every year there was a different person in charge.

In April 1980 John Egan was appointed Chairman and Chief Executive of Jaguar with the task of improving the Jaguar business and continuing the process of re-establishing it as a separately identifiable operation.

During 1980 the company passed through a critical period. Forty per cent of employees became redundant in order to make the organization viable. 'Mediocre' managers were replaced and after the cut backs, morale building campaigns were initiated for the remaining employees.

By the end of 1982 Jaguar's reputation for setting high standards of quality and reliability was well on the way to being re-established and demand had increased, particularly in the United States. The increased demand was matched by increased production rates and a favourable exchange rate generated a substantially better trading performance. In August 1984, the company became private again. Since then, it has been a matter of expanding to compete with the main competitors: BMW, Mercedes and Porsche.

During 1986 Jaguar recruited 1,385 new employees to support the expansion of key areas of the company. 'It was a successful year for the company' said John Egan in the 1987 Annual Report.

Founder's and leaders' values

As Watson (1963) argues, the corporation is the expression of those who have given it leadership in development and in the conduct of its affairs. The enduring truths of personal conduct, learned by the company's founder and past leaders have served as management guidelines in the development of the organization (Schein, 1983). This seems to be specially true for this case study.

Jaguar's founder is remembered as an 'ambitious man' from the earliest days of his enterprise. He combined drive and energy with a shrewd business brain. He was an 'autocratic boss' who rarely bothered with board meetings and is famous for calling everyone by his/her surname. His greatest quality was his 'eye for style'. He understood the importance of style and all his products had it.

The Chairman at the time of research was perceived by the managers as holding similar values to those of the founder. Jaguar's management perceive their culture as a clear reflection of their 'charismatic current leader'. The 'personality' of the organization coincided with the 'personality' of the Chairman. Both were described as: full of enthusiasm, energy and drive; active, prepared to accept any challenge. These values were reflected in the management of careers. Hence, the organization tended to select and promote dynamic, enthusiastic, energetic managers.

Jaguar's prevailing culture

Jaguar's top executives (both Personnel and Strategic Directors) involved in organizational change believed that the starting point for any necessary cultural modifications was to gain insight into the existing culture. In this particular case, this took the following form: a strong feeling of belonging, a desire to succeed and close identification with the product. These have been some of the employees' shared values in Jaguar from its creation (1922) until 1989, when the interviews were conducted.

Jaguar's existing culture was seen by the managers I interviewed as very traditional. For example, as they well described, the managers tended to use traditional methods of work - resisting both new technologies and also innovative personnel management practices. They described the Human Resource Department as having a 'macho type of philosophy'.

> You are supposed to work many hours and be seen to be very active. A deviant manager is the one who does not look "a hard worker"... Some managers still believe that just money motivates people to work.

For most of the managers the social environment is seen as being like a 'family'. 'It is informal, and we all feel part of the company as members of the family'. The recruitment policies in the past used to encourage families of employees to apply for jobs in the company.

Jaguar was thought by the managers I interviewed to be typical of many engineering organizations. They hired a high proportion of engineers to fill available management posts in different areas (production, purchase, finance, human resources). These engineers tended to be highly skilled in numerical and technical disciplines. However, the top executives felt that these graduates lacked the commercial skills needed to deal with an increasingly competitive external environment. One of them said: 'our culture is characterized by commercial naivety'.

The group I interviewed saw themselves as individualists:

> Managers are promoted if they are good in their own jobs rather than if they work in co-operation with other areas.

There was a tendency for different departments to work in isolation. A car industry, as perceived by the senior strategic manager, requires a team worker attitude in order to carry out most of its activities.

Although the style of management was described as varying in different sub sectors of the organization, a particular trait seemed to be predominant in these different sub cultures: the authoritarian. Managers were expected to be 'hard but fair'. The organization expected a good employee to do what he was told. As stated by a manager: 'It is necessary to be very persistent to get new ideas implemented.'

It might be a reflection of the transitional cultural phase that, by 1989, Jaguar was viewed as having a split personality. Externally it was identified with the product. There existed a general image of a high profile, dynamic, energetic, extrovert, sophisticated and luxury type of organization. But internally the image was different. It was that of a young organization, trying to find its own way, it was like 'an adolescent', indecisive about its future.

Jaguar's appropriate culture

Jaguar had achieved a stage of development where it found that some elements of its culture have become dysfunctional. Hence, the organization was exploring the possibility of evaluating and changing its culture to make it fit with the new business objectives.

Essential values were identified and preserved: loyalty, close identification with the product and a strong desire to succeed. There were, however, some vital elements of the culture which were not compatible with the new organization objectives, such as: tradition (rather than innovation), rigid attitudes, one way communication, emphasis on results (rather than on the process) and a reactive rather than an interactive attitude in communications with peers.

In order to promote the desired organizational changes, top management had decided to implement a company wide strategy called 'TQM' Total Quality Management. However, it failed as it did not fit with the corporate culture.

As perceived by top executives in Jaguar, people would manage in the future without fear of making mistakes. They would try out new ways of improving the job. They would be able to work in teams and co-operate within the organization. They would be more open about constant changes. They would listen more to the employees. They would be more flexible in their attitudes. They would show more ability to revise plans, and consider alternatives which would allow greater adaptability to cope with new work situations.

Most of the managers I interviewed thought that the type of managerial attitude which was appropriate when the company was public was then inappropriate for the organization to cope with the new environmental demands following privatization. Different eras demand different skills and abilities.

The analysis of managerial careers

The current career management in Jaguar clearly reflected the transitional phase the company was going through in its culture change process: The conflict of 'old' and 'new' values.

The management development

Historically, career planning in Jaguar was based on 'specialists'. Careers were vertically developed. No cross department or rotating jobs were encouraged. However, as perceived by top executives, to fit the appropriate culture, a manager needed to be a generalist. Hence, the current management development programme's main objective was to give the managers an opportunity to rotate and work in different departments. By submitting themselves to this development programme, the managers would acquire a broader view of their own business. This broader new knowledge of the organization would help them in the decision making process. It was expected that this programme would lead the executives to a less individualistic approach when managing their own areas. Additionally, managers were encouraged to undertake an MBA part time course. This part of the programme aimed to help managers in their process of changing from being pure specialists to becoming a more generalist type of professional. The career development programme, therefore, was intended to reinforce the new culture by giving a positive demonstration of what is expected from people's attitudes.

The managerial selection and promotion

The modifications of criteria for selecting and promoting managers have been made at a much slower rate than changes in management training and development. This resistance to modifying certain criteria was explained by

37

the managers as a consequence of the tradition of the firm. They have 'inherited' this type of system.

In the preparation for privatization (1983/1984), Jaguar brought into the organization people with the necessary experience and qualification - 'expertise' - to undertake specific managerial posts which were created as a consequence of privatization. However, they overlooked the candidate's values, for example, capacity for team work and openness to new ideas and innovation.

In the past, the main criteria used in decisions about hiring or promoting managers were the candidate's high level of IQ and his/her technical qualifications together with the number of years of experience in the motor car industry. The type of candidate considered right for Jaguar in the past also had to be energetic, dynamic and active. These characteristics were a clear reflection of the prevailing corporate culture.

It is interesting to note that the process of assessing the potential of managers had become more sophisticated over the past few years. However, the system in itself still reinforced the 'old values'. Hence, the assessment centre aimed to evaluate the managers' attitudes and behaviour through psychological tests, role playing and interviews. This in-house programme consisted of observing the manager under different situations. Although it was a new design programme, the final individual report was based on the analysis of certain characteristics which were considered relevant for the 'old culture' (drive, energy, dynamism, influence). The leadership style required for the managers to fit the new culture was participative, explained the top managers. However, this final report seemed to look for managers who still used their own charismatic powerful influence to get the work done. This programme, according to the managers' accounts, had not yet been modified to convey the new values and attitudes. There was, therefore, a split situation: top executives urged a change in management attitudes in order to cope with the current fluid situation that the organization faced. A more proactive and interactive team work was required, rather than a reactive management group: managers with more open attitudes, a less traditional style of management, executives who could listen to the employees, instead of expecting that the subordinates obey them blindly. Nevertheless, new personnel procedures which foster these new values had not yet been fully implemented.

Discussion

Jaguar's top management were concerned about how to change the organization's culture in order to adapt to new environmental constraints.

Jaguar's historical culture was appropriate when the economic conditions were more favourable: better exchange rates (US$ and £), mild market competition; financial support from the government. By 1989, however, the costs of the product were too high, with the company unable to compete successfully in the market place. The only 'way out' senior managers foresaw for the company's survival, without a takeover, was to replace gradually some of their working values: for example, from authoritarian to a more participative style of management; from engineering biased to commercially oriented; from traditional to innovative (see figure 6).

	Prevailing		**Appropriate**
Culture:	• dynamism • technically biased • individualist • authoritarian/traditional • formality • enthusiasm	Culture:	• commercially oriented • team work • participative/innovative

Careers:	• managers as specialists
	• individualism
	• authoritarian
	  management style
	• dynamic managers
		Careers:	• managers as generalists
			  (business oriented - MBA)
			• cooperation
			• participative management
			  style
			• thoughtful managers

Figure 6 Culture change and managerial careers: Jaguar Cars

However, all the managers interviewed saw the organization's culture as not actually in the process of change. The 'appropriate' culture was described as the 'desired' one. Nevertheless, how to get there from here seemed to be the problem in Jaguar.

Managers revealed that the CEO style of management and consequently the 'role modelling' was the key barrier in the culture change process in Jaguar. Furthermore, the systems which communicated and reinforced management attitudes had not yet been modified according to the 'new culture'. New managers were being selected (from outside) and being evaluated under 'old' or 'historical' criteria. The only sub system which had changed was training and development. However, management training and development activities in isolation do not stimulate the necessary changes in the managerial behaviour.

Conclusions

This case study has explored the impact of culture change on managerial careers in Jaguar. It first explained how culture was created: founder's values (authoritarianism, formality, enthusiasm) and the type of industry (individualism, technically biased) represent predominant factors in it.

The need for a culture change in Jaguar stemmed from the following environmental factors:

1 fiercer market competition (e.g. the Japanese luxury cars).

2 instability in the exchange rates (US$ and £).

3 less financial support from the government since the company became privatized in 1984.

In their battle to survive, Jaguar management were trying to become more commercially oriented than engineering biased. In this process of culture change, however, the required modifications in career management process were slower than expected. This seemed to represent a barrier in the change process.

Jaguar's top executives were gradually recognizing the strong links between corporate culture and managerial careers. However, there appeared to be a distinctive time lag between realization and implementation of such necessary changes in career management which slowed down the required process of organizational/culture change.

Notes

1. Jaguar was sold to Ford in 1989.

British Nuclear Fuels Ltd (BNFL) case study

The problem

British Nuclear Fuels is a state enterprise. Since its creation and up to 1971, BNFL was financially and politically supported by the Government. Since 1971, however, BNFL's financial resources come either from their clients or from financial institutions. The company is gradually becoming more independent of the Government and working more internationally. Following the current UK Government policies, the company is a candidate for privatization. However, as stated by the chairman, Christopher Harding:

> Quite a few problems have to be resolved first, mainly, we need a change of culture.

Background

British Nuclear Fuels (BNFL) is the most experienced nuclear fuel company in the world, having supplied nuclear fuel cycle services in the UK and overseas for over forty years. BNFL supplies the fuel for the UK's nuclear power programme which produces around a fifth of the country's electricity. In addition, a substantial export business has been developed with nuclear power plant operators in Western Europe, Japan and North America, which now accounts for eighteen per cent of the annual turnover.

The company employs over 15,000 people, with estimated additional jobs in the UK's construction and manufacturing industries supported by BNFL's massive £5.5 billion programme of investment over the next decade. In 1988 the company spent £750 million on goods and services.

Location

BNFL's plants are situated in North West England and Southern Scotland. Nuclear fuel and fuel products are manufactured at Springfields near Preston, uranium enrichment by the centrifuge process is carried out at Capenhurst near Chester, and reprocessing and waste management services are based at Sellafield in West Cumbria. The company's headquarters and engineering design facilities are at Risley near Warrington. BNFL also owns and operates two nuclear power stations - at Calder Hall on the Sellafield site and at Chapelcross in southern Scotland.

41

This case description covers two periods:

a)   the historical or 'stagnation period' - from 1971 to 1984
b)   the prevailing period - from 1984 to 1989

The prevailing period starts with the appointment of a new chairman, Christopher Harding, ushering the organization into an era of major strategic overall changes in its battle to survive.

> The new chairman was introduced to BNFL early in 1984 by the Department of Energy, eager to bring new blood to the board of its troubled company.

A new CEO, Mr. Neville Chamberlain and also a new General Manager for Sellafield (the site which employs the largest proportion - ninety per cent - of the work force), were appointed subsequently by the Chairman.

Sellafield was chosen to be investigated, as this site is responsible for ninety per cent of the work force and at the time of investigation (1989) was considered by top management as in the process of 'major culture change'.

The need for a culture change

According to the Human Resources Director (Risley - HQ), during the last few years the organization has been going through a major process of change mainly as a result of:

a)   a more competitive international market
b)   the possibility of privatization

The need for major change has gradually emerged over the last decade and is primarily concerned with commercial environmental factors. As said by a senior manager:

> BNFL is becoming increasingly commercial.

As senior managers stated, the company's *mission* is now:

a)   to assure that nuclear generating electricity in the UK is competitive with other sources of electricity generation
b)   to become internationally competitive, because its main customer, CEGB, is starting to buy energy from abroad

From 1971 to 1984 was a very stagnant period for organizational change in BNFL. This can be illustrated by the Human Resources Director.

42

> We had a main captive customer, CEGB... Most of our contracts were customer based - "costs plus profits". The actual cost to run the company plus a "mark up" for profits determined the selling price of the product. In such a system, there were no incentives for the organization to reduce its costs let alone to become more efficient. Therefore, while BNFL was a monopoly supplier to the UK generating boards, prices were agreed at a cost plus basis.

Whereas, in the past, there was no external pressure forcing the company to innovate, the picture has become different as a consequence of external pressures. To quote a senior manager:

> If the company has to join a scramble for orders, it must be able to quote fixed competitive prices comparable with those obtainable elsewhere in the world, and look to its operations to ensure a reasonable profit.

BNFL's services were comparatively expensive and its customers were reluctant to pay these rates. If the company did not become more efficient, it would have lost its customers to France or other major competitors.

The historical culture in Sellafield: 1971 to 1984

BNFL's culture has been inherited from the Civil Service. The historical values and assumptions reinforced the concept of a 'benevolent' organization where the core mission was not to be profitable. Rather, the core *mission* in the past was:

> ...to offer jobs to the community and be technically perfect as a scientific type of firm.

Managers perceived Sellafield in the past to be a very pleasant working place. There was lack of competitiveness and an enjoyable working environment. Managers' perception of Sellafield was that of an organization which was not willing to change or create new working methods. Traditional in management practices, the company was considered as 'old fashioned' in its way of managing people, tasks and money. According to managers, this 'slow' pace of improving management practices is linked to the type of industry BNFL is in. That is, because of the long life of Sellafield's waste products, it is difficult to respond rapidly to change. From the conception of a plant to the start of the operation is at least twenty years. Hence, the process of change is slow.

> It would be easier to respond to change if we made dish washers.

Although described as a 'static' organization as regards management's new practices, Sellafield was considered very dynamic in developing new technologies directly linked to the quality of their products or services. BNFL, like the whole nuclear industry is characterized by almost 'continuous small step technical improvement'. Thus, the concern of BNFL managers in

43

the past was technical excellence: 'Let's do it right'. Every time the managers saw some small thing to improve, the attitude was the following: 'Let's change it', either the product or the service. It did not matter too much what the cost of the change would be. Management agreed that Sellafield had a reputation for a high level of achievement in the service they offered.

Sellafield was like an 'old fashioned doctor', 'an expert', an 'old fashioned specialist', technically competent but holding old fashioned ideas. BNFL was also seen as a 'secretive organization'.

> The culture of the civil service doesn't tell people what they need to know. Sellafield was like a mysterious person holding a lot of secrets. Everybody in this organization knows what we mean by "the need to know" philosophy.

Another trait revealed by managers in describing the personality of Sellafield was 'benevolent', 'tolerant'. The organization was considered benevolent and tolerant mainly as regards spending money and costs. For example, in the past, travelling expenses were not tightly controlled. For instance, if a manager had to do a work trip, taxi expenses were not controlled as they are today.

Sellafield was very bureaucratic. The ability to write was an important requirement of management skills as it was reinforced by the historical appraisal system.

Historical leadership style

Managers in Sellafield, and the rest of BNFL used to have a 'job for life'. They felt secure and relaxed; they were under no pressure concerning overall organizational results. Employees at Sellafield used to work from 8.30 a.m. to 4.00 p.m. and also had long coffee breaks. This attitude reflected the very relaxed managerial attitude of the past. 'We were not committed to the company's results'.

Managers, in the past, lived under a non innovative, low risk system. 'All had to be safe at all costs'. BNFL was viewed as low risk system:

> Although security was not essential in ninety nine per cent of what we did, the philosophy of safety, stemming from the inherent dangers of the nuclear industry, seemed to affect management attitudes in all other situations

Following the belief in a high level of security, managers were also discouraged from new ideas in day to day activities. To fit the old corporate culture, in the past, managers were required to 'obey' the system. However, some managers, in isolation, eventually acted in an innovative way. They would be supported only if their ideas were successful.

> You are OK if you get success. But, if you get one or two failures, you get knocked down. People will remember your failure and I hope this attitude is starting to change.

44

Line managers on plant were considered to have responsibility but, very often, no authority. This is best illustrated by the quotation:

> I am allowed a lot of freedom in one way in terms of the technical part of my job, but I am not allowed freedom in terms of the way I manage my staff... it is regimented... it is all negotiable elsewhere... I don't consider myself a manager really.

The delegation process was poor. As a manager says:

> You have to report back all the time to your superiors, as opposed to management at lower levels. Everybody wants to check. They are over conscientious, those who are working for them.

There was a very bureaucratic management attitude. 'We tended to follow the rules'. For example, if the finance department did not allow the manager freedom of choice, then he would find a way to obey the system. It was an inflexible management system. 'Like a brick wall'. A senior executive in Sellafield has described the past managerial attitude as a 'policeman'. It was important *just* to make sure that the rules were obeyed.

The communications between senior managers and the rest of the organization were very poor:

> ...they (senior managers) kept sending notes through the post instead of talking with managers... "I never met the senior manager!!", a middle manager said twice.

To summarize, there follows the descriptions of *The Historical Personality of Sellafield:*

> As a person, Sellafield was very slow. This person, in the past, reminded me of an elephant. He didn't want to move or change, not a challenging person... he would not improve, innovate... we were not a good proven system in management terms.

> It is like a piece of machinery. A big wheel rolling along. It is like a lumbering bureaucratic giant. Old, lethargic, not a dynamic organization.

> ...a very academic person: a perfectionist, over conscientious, not very flexible. A dogmatic person who enjoys living under many rules.

Among the very rich and expressive statements that managers came out with during the interviews, I found the one below most representative in reflecting the historical organizational mission.

> Sellafield, in the past, looked like a social rugby team which goes out and tries to win but, basically, wanted to have a good game. Everybody tried hard, but at the end of the day it did not matter very much as long as you had a good game.

The historical managerial career systems

This section explores the values and beliefs implicitly expressed in personnel practices. It was clear that personnel practices in the past reflected the historical culture of BNFL. The personnel department has always kept a very strong administrative role: 'Rigid structures and well established systems'.

> Personnel practices in the civil service are like the military system. Nothing was negotiable, there was no flexibility in personnel procedures at all. For example, people still take leave, they do not go on holiday. There was no negotiation between top management and the other levels within the organization.

Management selection/promotion/development

Personnel function's main role, in the past, was the recruitment and selection of graduates.

> I don't think personnel officers choose people for the company, except for the graduates.

They selected graduates from public schools and Oxford and Cambridge. The graduates were usually chosen by academic qualification. The best were briefly interviewed and assessed by 'feeling', 'intuition' or by identifying 'clones', people with similar backgrounds and outlook. The criteria for choosing the graduates (in fact, the future managers) were based solely on technical competence and academic qualifications.

Sellafield had a very low employee turnover. It tended to prepare their own managers by providing young graduates with the appropriate on the job technical training. As a consequence, today, such managers lack business experience and, in addition, they 'have never been exposed to real managerial roles'.

Managers were promoted to replace people immediately above them, rarely to replace managers in other places or departments. They were promoted largely according to seniority. The ultimate questions used to be: 'How old are you? How long have you been doing your job for?' It was a very subjective assessment, very personal. The promotion decision depended on the senior managers and on what their criteria were. There were no overall company criteria. The profile of managers located in different departments reflected the senior managers' values in that department.

Every post and layer of management was filled and managers would argue that the importance of the job could be seen by the number of employees located below them. In fact, managers in that old structure had small jobs. According to some, this system was faulty because even if there were no vacancy, but a person was considered ready for promotion, she or he would be promoted. Consequently, 'we created a very fat organization, with too many people'.

A manager who 'got on' in Sellafield had the following characteristics: technically competent, tolerant with people, personable (a good chap), experienced in the area, and capable in writing.

It is interesting to note that different sub systems in 'historical' managerial careers were reinforcing a bureaucratic culture.

> If you did your job efficiently you did not get noticed. However, if you used to write lots of reports, at least you would become recognized by senior managers... Certainly, if you did catch the right people's attention (senior managers) you were bound to be promoted.

As regards the profile of a deviant manager in the old days, it was clear that creativity was regarded as negative. Some managers described the deviant manager as follows:

> People who had opinions which contradicted their bosses. Someone who sticks his neck out, or is adventurous in terms of management style, i.e. let's try this, let's try that...That attitude tended to represent a block to their promotion.

Management development was considered poor in the past. Graduates were given a pre-structured two year on the job training. The objectives of this training were mainly to update them in technical aspects of the industry. After these two years, however, they would be left on their own. They would be stuck in the structure, working for many years at the same job, and 'decades on the same site'.

Thus, the usual thought in the past was:

> I have been working for many years in this job, on this site. I want to continue here.

Consequently, the senior management in the company today encounter difficulties in identifying managers who are prepared either to replace people who are retiring or to fill new jobs as the organization is expanding. For example, it is very common to find managers at grade twelve (high in the hierarchy) who have a very narrow experience in the company. They have been working for ten/twelve years on the same site, doing the same job. They know everything about their plant, but their knowledge about other areas of the organization is very limited. Moreover, these people have locked the information within themselves rather than in the system. Thus, there is a belief that 'if we moved these people (who have been there for ten/twelve years) to other departments, their original sectors would collapse'.

Historical management appraisal and rewards

As a reflection of a secretive historical culture (as explained earlier), managers in Sellafield were secretive about careers, jobs, and money. The payment system was purely a function of the length of time managers had worked for the organization. 'If you did a good or bad job you would still get the same pay'... The structure was viewed as very rigid. Managers were not allowed to negotiate salaries with their employees.

> If I wanted to give more money to someone who did a particularly good job, I had no authority for that.

As a reflection of the 'non achieving' past culture, the 'historical' appraisal was not connected with performance.

> Managers would be paid whether or not they were committed and contributed at a high or low level to the results of the company.

Historically the appraisal system was not regarded as important. It was just one more paper to be filled in. It was like a school report. The manager had to comment on different aspects of an employee's behaviour, such as: how he gets on with colleagues and superiors (reflecting a very conforming type of expected managerial behaviour), and writing abilities (reflecting the bureaucratic culture). According to managers, the appraisal system was subjective, and reminded them of a 'clerical' system. In this process, managers were very reluctant to make any negative or derogatory comments which could risk their relationship with their staff. 'It was easier to keep the staff happy in this way'. It seems that the appraisal system, in the past, was reinforcing a benevolent and bureaucratic culture .

The transitional phase of BNFL culture change process: from the 'old' to the 'new' culture

BNFL was passing through a transitional phase of culture change. As such, there was a conflict situation of two cultures an old and a new. Sellafield was described by managers as 'schizophrenic':

> We can perceive two cultures in one. Some people fight not to change. Others are fighting to change... i.e. a number of people are trying to push the organization off the civil service course into a more competitive type of organization, others are blocking this process.

In the past, BNFL offered 'a job for life'. Hence, the average age of a manager today is relatively high. Many of them are now near retirement. These people tend to resist change. This situation was well explained by a manager who has been working for BNFL for over forty years.

> If you are a senior manager and have just four or five years to work before retirement, you really don't care about implementing changes. You just sit at your desk and wait for your pension. Whereas if you are twenty years younger, you are still keen on getting promoted.

Consequently, while the older managers complain about the high speed of organizational change, most of the young managers seem to be frustrated with the slow rate of change.

> The company is moving very quickly, according to some old managers. The young ones are more impatient, for them we are moving very slowly...

According to the young managers, the majority of people in BNFL used to work in a very 'slow way':

> If you push hard, they feel very uncomfortable within the new rhythm... We are much more under stress, we have to justify our position much more. We have to justify our own contribution ... We have got to be committed.

BNFL new culture (1984 to 1989)

Sellafield has changed from its emphasis on research and development and on technological improvement to being a business enterprise. The main preoccupation is now on how to run the organization. Most of the historical values described in the previous section have become dysfunctional as the organization faces a highly competitive business environment. Today BNFL is struggling to replace some of the 'civil service' practices. The new top management are aware that developing a new culture to reinforce competitiveness is a necessary task for organizational survival.

> BNFL's civil service origins have left their mark, and we are having to expunge them in order that the organization may prosper in a wholly commercial environment.

Senior managers perceive more clearly the changes in corporate values, beliefs and, consequently, management attitudes. They are, in fact, agents for change, and thus, more sensitive to change. Middle managers, however, have difficulty in identifying major changes in day to day organizational life.

According to them, 'the company is trying to become different', but 'there is a long way to go to change our culture'. 'We are very far from being what we need to be'.

Sellafield was seen, in the past, as a benevolent organization regarding costs and results. Today, however, the managers as a whole, are gradually becoming more aware of the need to cut costs: cost of people, cost of activities, cost of change, are all issues with which managers are concerned. The organization is becoming more concerned with achievement and there is an increasing need for managers to understand and identify with business plans. Whereas in the past the technological plans were vital, now business plans are the main concern. Managers are gradually developing a much clearer idea of what their group, section, department is expected to achieve to further the business plan of the organization. They are receiving better information to enable them to make their managerial decisions which are connected to a larger plan. Decisions are now based on business objectives.

> We have to make our decisions based on balance: safety, R&D and commercial issues.

To summarize the process of culture change in BNFL, from historical to prevailing culture, I will quote the statements managers used to describe the BNFL *prevailing personality*:

While the personality of Sellafield yesterday was perceived as 'relaxing', it is now seen as 'restless'. Ten years ago, this organization was perceived as 'static', and 'technically competent'. Today, the corporate image is different. Sellafield is perceived by employees as more 'dynamic', with 'lots of drive' and 'determination'. Contrary to the 'policeman' of yesterday, Sellafield's senior managers today see themselves as 'citizens'. One of them tried to explain this metaphor:

> We try to understand the rules of the system instead of just following them, because, at the end of the day, to win the rugby match is what now matters in Sellafield.

Prevailing leadership style (desired culture)

The style of senior managers' leadership has changed significantly. They are now trying to innovate and to find new ways to do the job. They are more aware of their own role as businessmen. 'We are becoming less bureaucratic', said a senior manager.

> Today, if the system does not work, we ask why? We ask: How could we bend the rules to suit the company needs? What can we do in order to make sure the company gets value for money in any decision... Now we need fewer rules... fewer policies... broad policies are enough for senior managers to make business decisions.

Attention to subcultures is an important issue. Nevertheless, some core managerial profiles are the same for all management jobs:

1   flexibility to work in a changeable environment.

2   capacity to understand the historical culture and ability to gradually implement changes in the direction of a desired or 'appropriate' culture.

Top management are aware that a full understanding of the organization's own stages of development and its own ingrained values and beliefs, and also its sub cultures (on different sites) is necessary for a successful managerial performance.

The new managerial careers systems

In the past, decisions on managerial careers were localised and reflected various senior managers' criteria. Now, top management realise the need for a corporate strategy for managerial careers.

> We need a very strong direction from Headquarters. We need a corporate strategy for career systems in order to assure the appropriate pattern of management behaviour and to control the quality of our managers' selections...

> We should not rely on the system today to say who has potential or not, because it is very personal.

Top management involved in organizational change believe that to achieve adequate culture change, a lot of the 'old' personnel systems need to be replaced.

> Some of the old personnel practices have already gone. But, there is still a long way to go for organizational survival.

According to the Career Development Manager, the impact of major organization changes on career systems is mainly:

a) we need to reduce the staff, make the organization slimmer, and
b) *we need to get the right people for the job*. (his emphasis)

The philosophy of prevailing career systems is well expressed by a senior line manager at Sellafield:

> To win the rugby game, we need to choose the players carefully and place them in strategic positions...

And also by a Human Resources top executive in BNFL at Risley (HQ):

> W need to learn how to identify people's skills better, we need to be more skilful in managing people we need to be wonderful leaders.

According to this senior executive, to become 'wonderful leaders' implies a radical change in management attitudes. In answering my question about how to change management attitudes, he replied:

1   by rotating them (placing managers in different areas for a pre-established period of time)
2   by setting an example (ensuring that the top management attitudes are appropriate), and
3   by rewarding by results (implementing new appraisal and promotional systems)

For the last few years, there has been a tendency to recruit managers from outside the organization. Top management are gradually recognizing that people from related industries can bring essential skills to the organization. Sellafield is no longer selecting people on technical expertise alone. Nowadays they look for the following in the candidates: communication skills, leadership qualities (leading to a solution via group decision making), problem solving, adaptability and mainly *how they react to change*.

To reach the top, a manager needs to understand three to five major areas in the company. There are, therefore, more cross site placements. To 'get on' today, managers need to understand the financial implications of each decision and also the implications of any decision in other areas.

Managers agree that the old rules for placing people in different jobs were too rigid. Certain jobs were only regarded as suitable for people with first or second class degrees. In many cases, however, they realized that people with lower educational achievements would be better at some jobs than better qualified graduates.

The company is now making efforts to introduce more competition among managers. There is less job security, people no longer feel they have a 'job for life'. At the moment there is some instability as the organization is reducing its number of staff.

The modifications in senior management selection and promotion represented the priority action towards culture change process in BNFL. Historically, managers were assessed by their technical skills. Today, a general expertise is required from managers to 'get up' the career ladder.

While in the past length of experience was an important criterion for senior managers' promotion, today the individual's attitudes are more relevant. Deviant managers of the past (those who were willing to implement new ideas) are being promoted to senior positions as the criteria for selecting/promoting managers have changed.

In November 1988, top executives at the Risley HQ, together with the Career Development Department, developed a consensus regarding the profile of a future BNFL senior manager. A new career development system has been implemented on an experimental corporate basis. This system tries to identify future managers to meet the requirements of the different sites. During the assessment centres, senior personnel managers, external consultants, senior line managers and directors act as referees to evaluate the manager's potential.

BNFL's criteria for promoting senior managers today seem to differ significantly from those described in the historical promotion system. The company is now looking for people who are able 'to create the rules instead of following the rules'. A recently promoted senior executive says:

> I was considered a rebel some years ago, a deviant. Now, I am a senior manager.

More dynamic and creative people are now being promoted to senior posts. One example of that was the appointment of the new managing director for Sellafield. The new managing director has been working for BNFL for twenty years in various positions. Recently (1987) he was promoted by the new chairman. The new GM for Sellafield is considered a 'charismatic' and 'participative' leader and his predecessor was considered a 'very quiet and reserved' manager. It is recognized by management that expected managerial behaviour is changing. To 'get on' now and in the future, a manager should assume responsibility for the results in his area of responsibility. They should address the problems themselves, i.e. they ought to be able to say: 'This is my problem', instead of avoiding it, using the defence mechanism which, according to managers, was the typical 'historical' managerial behaviour.

The profile of a good manager is summarized in the following manager's words:

> The key thing is the ability to live with change. For this, a manager ought to be self confident and able to propose different ideas. His ability to cope with change and work in a fluid situation is extremely relevant. Great emphasis is given to communication skills because, in a changing situation, the need to communicate is greater than in a static situation when the things do not change over years and years (if you stay always doing the same job, you do not need to explain anything to anybody)... Commercial awareness, enthusiasm, (in order to facilitate the process of changing habits in people...). Initiative, ability to get things done, accepting responsibility and delegating responsibility...

A deviant manager today is described by managers as a contemplative person, 'slavish', sticking to old ideas.

Management appraisal and rewards

According to top managers involved in the culture change process, the appraisal system is a critical subsystem of managerial career systems because it represents an effective vehicle to communicate the new organizational values. However, as expected with a culture change, this process has been implemented gradually in BNFL. New appraisal and reward systems have been implemented only at senior levels.

Contrary to the secretive nature of 'historical' managerial behaviour, the communications over an individual's performance have been more effective over the last few years. There is more openness. However, 'This is only a small move', says a manager.

There is a great demand for performance, for results. Now there is pressure towards better managerial achievement. It implies a demand for greater output in each area. The method the organization uses to judge performance is still purely number based: 'Same number of people, doing more work'.

It seems to contrast with the historical reward system in which managers salaries were linked to the number of staff they were responsible for. Today it is the contrary. For example, explained a senior manager 'I manage fewer people today than before my promotion to senior management'.

As observed by senior managers, these new criteria for appraisal and reward based upon performance have not yet been applied to middle managers and the lower levels. The existing appraisal and reward system for these levels still reinforces the old organizational values. However, for senior managers it reinforces new organizational values.

	Historical		**Prevailing**
Mission:	• offer jobs to the community • be safe	**Mission:**	• be a commercial organization • be safe
Culture:	• safety • secrecy • technically biased • bureaucratic, paternalism	**Culture:**	• business oriented • valuing management skills • valuing innovation
Careers:	• towards specialisation • slow career moves • rewarding by seniority • conformity	**Careers:**	• towards 'general' expertise - MBA • faster career moves • performance related rewards • initiative, creativity, flexibility

Figure 7 Culture change and managerial careers: BNFL

BNFL's process of change appears to be consistent (across functions) and gradual and to employ a participatory style of management to lead it. In the process of implementing a more participatory management style, some managers in Sellafield decided to reshape the organization structure. This was considered a tool to be used by BNFL senior managers in order to change their culture, 'we are nearer the employees than before'. Thus, a two way communication would be facilitated. According to top management, the new organizational structure that some departments are experimenting with, seems to be very efficient in provoking changes in attitudes. This new structure aims to cut down the number of levels in the hierarchical organization.

British Airways (BA) case study

Introduction

> Today, increasingly, any airline can fly any route wherever they like. So, we came from a highly regulated industry to a highly deregulated industry. That is why the need for change started...

In the early days of British Airways, civil aviation was very much regulated between different countries. The industry then started to move towards a more deregulated business. As stated by Bruce (1987):

> Complexity, turbulence and geographical distance are critical features of the operating environment for BA today. At the same time, deregulation, with fierce competition for markets, is breaking up the comfortable cartel of earlier years (pp. 21-26).

As a consequence of market deregulation, British Airways was facing gradually increasing international competition. Thus, there was a need for a change from a technically biased organizational culture towards a commercially or market oriented culture.

> The airline was inward looking. We were insulated, we did not recognize competition, it was an introverted culture which did not focus itself outside.

Consequently, early in 1985, BA became financially nonviable as a business. At that time, the company was protected by the Government. The possibility of privatization exposed the company's unprofitability.

A briefing on BA

British Airways is one of the world's largest international airlines. Its principal activities are the operation of international and domestic scheduled and charter air services for the carriage of passengers and cargo. In August 1989 BA group employed 40,252 staff, 29,000 of whom were located in the London area, mainly at Heathrow Airport, over 5,000 in other UK locations and another 5,000 overseas.

History

British Airways can trace its origins back to the pioneering days of civil aviation after the First World War.

The world's first daily international scheduled air service commenced on 25 August 1919 and was operated by Aircraft Transport and Travel Limited, which was combined in 1924 with a number of other privately owned air transport companies to form Imperial Airways Limited. A number of smaller UK air transport companies merged in 1935 to form the original privately owned British Airways Limited, which became Imperial Airways' principal UK competitor on its European routes.

Following a Government review, Imperial Airways and British Airways were nationalized in 1939 to form BOAC. In 1946, BEA was established as a separate statutory corporation to take over and develop the European services of BOAC. BEA also developed a domestic network to various points in the United Kingdom.

From 1946 until 1960 there were two Government run airlines in the UK: BOAC (for long routes) and BEA (for Europe). In 1973, BOAC and BEA were merged to form British Airways (BA). The merger of BEA and BOAC had left the airline overstaffed with duplicated tasks and with a low sense of identity within the company.

> This first culture change was a significant exercise in itself ... It was really painful for most of us.

After that, BA hadn't changed that much until 1984 when Colin Marshall the new chief executive officer, came and prepared the company for privatization. This case describes the BA culture in two periods:

1973 to 1984, the 'old culture'
1984 to 1989, the 'new culture'

The major process of planned change started in 1984. This date coincides with the privatization decision (April, 1984) and with the appointment of the CEO, BA was privatized in 1987.

The historical period: 1973 to 1984, the 'old' culture

The old mission

British Airways' mission, in the past, was to be an efficient airline operating company. To keep the aircraft flying in a safe way was the chief aim of the organization.

> We couldn't get away from the fact that we were running an operation. The operation was everything. The customers were just an unfortunate add on.

BA's new CEO understood the need to clarify the organization's past and the appropriate values for the future. He diagnosed the situation as follows:

> BA was an organization that did not really understand the word profit, that was very fearful of moving into the private sector... It was also obvious to me that the organization was extremely introverted, had really no grasp of what the marketplace wanted, what the customer wanted.

The idea is reinforced by a Senior Customers Manager:

> Before 1983, we were quite "arrogant", we tended to know what was the best for our customers. It was one of our beliefs that the customers didn't know what was the best for themselves (the manager laughs as if disagreeing with this past belief).

BA was designed around the armed forces. The people who originally ran the company moved from a military to a civil airline. It was a military type of culture:

> We used to have, until recently, a management dining room - the management mess - and the canteen for the other employees ...

It was a formal work environment:

> People in the past were called by their titles not by their names. The job titles would come first in any list of people.

Managers were also respected for their position and status within the organization.

The historical management style: inflexible, formal/bureaucratic, authoritarian The managerial behaviour expected in the past was too rigid and inflexible and the level of initiative required by managers was very low. Managers were expected to behave with a minimum of freedom as 'the rules of the game' were well written in manuals. It was considered a bureaucratic and formal work environment:

> We were, in the past, a bureaucratic organization, and highly hierarchical. There was a very strong sense of what was right or wrong, systems were very stable. Things happened in a particular way, behaviour was always very predictable. We had a big operating manual to dictate our behaviour... we were a management team which really had their hands tied behind their backs.

BA had a highly hierarchical organizational structure. BA employees did not have the opportunity to express their own views regarding working practices or any other issues.

> Communication was poor, and the lack of co-operation among areas was seen as a constraint on progress. In the old style of BA, each department was a fortress, and spent a lot of time battling against the other departments. Managers were not very visible to the staff. They never went out and talked to them.

There was a 'gulf between managers and the staff' in terms of communication.

The historical decision making There was a traditional hierarchical approach to problem solving in the airline, in which the 'task was handed down from A to B to C' (Bruce, 1987). Therefore, decisions were made in isolation, without involving other areas affected by the issue to be decided.

The historical management style in BA was 'too formal' which coincides with the former CEO's values:

> Our former CEO and chairman were different people if we compare them with the current ones. They were very distant from the staff. We, then, had different models to follow.

Another important trait of the historical management style, was the authoritarian and non participatory style of management which once again coincides with past leaders' values.

> The old managers preferred to tell people what to do instead of involving them in decisions. They also thought that it was a matter of status being far from the staff.

Prior to privatization, management style in the Engineering department was very aggressive, dictatorial, very autocratic and very domineering.

The historical managerial career systems

(Recruitment, selection, training and development, appraisal and rewards)

In the past, people were selected or promoted just to fill a position at that moment, not as part of future vision, or a career perspective. They were promoted because of their technical experience.

> In the old days, people were promoted when it was "their turn", when they were in the company for a certain number of years. It was common to hear this comment: I will be promoted in two years' time because it will be my turn.

Another criterion used for selecting and promoting managers was a reflection of the political environment: 'who knows whom?', 'who is a friend of whom?'.

Training activities were focused on developing skills for a specific task:

how to answer the phone, to
how to conduct an interview.

It was a very introvert organization, showing low or no interest in acquiring new technology.

We were very parochial. We didn't care about what was happening in other companies, in other industries or in other departments.

Managers' knowledge was limited to their own particular areas. The more senior they got, the better they became in their own particular areas.

For example, someone getting to the age of forty who has never experienced finance, marketing, production, people management, and so on. They had their careers limited. There are a large number of managers of that age with very narrow experience in the company.

Appraisal and reward systems in the past were unrelated to performance. Their goals were unclear for all managers:

Nobody would be given objectives or even feedback about how they were performing. The reward system was just by length of service. I have worked in this company since 1970, very rarely, somebody would talk to me about my performance. To give goals, never. You were always in the dark, you would ask yourself what is expected from you. When someone said "we do not like what you are doing" it was a big shock ... We thought we were humane. But we would have been more humane if we had given the chance for a person to change.

The appraisal system was considered political and subjective. There was no formal appraisal system. Departments used to have their own appraisal. Some departments never had appraisals. It was a localized decision, different parts of the airline used different methods to appraise their people.

This type of reward was unsatisfactory.

What motivation could you have, when you worked your fingers to the bone and the person in the next office just sat there, read the paper, drank coffee, and you both have the same kinds of rewards.

The prevailing period

The new mission

BA's core mission had changed from its focus on the operation to be customer focused.

Flying the aeroplane is now a part of the getting the business to work, not the thing that everybody needs to have experience in or be a professional in.

Customers are everything now, and the operation is subsidiary to the customers. There is a great emphasis on the primary purpose of the business: getting people to travel and to be pleased with their experience, and to come back several times.

New culture

When Lord King became chairman of BA in February 1981, he started to stress competition as a new value to be introduced in the organizational culture.

> My endeavours will be concentrated on doing all I can to see that British Airways has all the resources it requires to maintain and improve its standing as one of the greatest carriers in the world (quoted from Young, 1989).

> We aim to be the best and the most successful company in the fields of travel, tourism and transport.

Furthermore the front page of a BA News letter in 1989 quotes Lord King's statement:

> Once again we achieved record profits... we are in the forefront of the world's most profitable airlines, we are aware of the need for constant attention to costs.

Internal training programmes such as 'to be the best' also communicated the intention of BA to become more competitive.

Although different managers describe the new culture in different ways, they all agree that the historical values have been gradually and slowly changing. Both the managers who have worked for BA for twenty years and the newcomers, share this view. To quote a newcomer who had worked for BA for three years:

> The company is no doubt changing, slowly, changing for the better. I see the organization as having type A (business man) and type B (non business man) people. Type A is increasing in number. But, on a very slow basis. Type B are passengers, or workers, never managers, they are not thinking about the business at all, they are thinking about their own area, but not the business as a whole.

As a consequence of this new mission, a Customer Service department was created. Emphasis was placed on marketing activities and the quality of passenger handling was then highly valued compared with before.

> Customer surveys are more respected.

New managerial style Management style seems to be moving towards different directions in each area. Some areas, such as sales and marketing, are considered 'more open' and participatory than others, such as Engineering.

> We engineers were trained to be narrow minded

contrast, a sales manager's account:

> Today the management style is much more based on team work. It is not so important the position you are in, but the power of your argument.

An overall change:

Managers in a general way, feel freer to manage their own areas than they did before. Personal accountability seems to be more important than bureaucracy.

> We are exposing our abilities as managers... we had to put away the great operating manuals. Today we say to our staff: do not just complain about this, do something yourself, you know more than the manuals...

Informality among peers is gradually emerging in all areas of BA.

> Now there is more openness, more involvement. The staff are more ready to come up with new ideas.

The prevailing decision making Contrasting with the old style when decisions were made in isolation, within each department, it has become essential to get a consensus among different areas before deciding anything related to the business. Nevertheless, the transitional phase was leading the organization to the other extreme in the decision making process:

> If we were guilty in the past of not considering the implications of one decision in other areas, now we are guilty of taking too long to make decisions. Then, when we take it, it is with regard to everybody else but it is too late...

Differences of values and beliefs among departments (such as marketing, finance, engineering, etc.) represent a significant barrier to achieving a homogeneous new managerial style in the organization as a whole. Parts of the company which are exposed to our customers had to change very quickly. Other parts of the airline have hardly changed at all. Hence, there is a wide gap between departments. This gap seems to be a constraint in the process of communication among areas, making harder the decision making process, affecting ultimately the business achievements.

The prevailing managerial careers systems

In the past, managerial careers were made by opportunities arising. Today, it is about matching people and jobs. Therefore, a career planning programme specially designed for high flyers has been implemented.

The existing managerial selection, promotion, development and appraisal in British Airways have been restructured since 1984 when the new CEO launched a campaign to change BA culture. The aim was to replace some of the 'old values' with 'new ones'. In its effort to change its image, the Human Resource department replaced the Personnel department. Some managers considered that changing these titles was just a 'cosmetic' action, as the role of the department remained the same as in the past, to *control people*.

Job security is no longer an accepted value in BA. Staff and overheads were cut down radically in the early 1980s. The number of people was reduced by thirty per cent, from 50,000 to 35,000 employees. High instability among top management occurred as a consequence of the new human resource philosophy.

Eighty senior managers were asked to take early retirement. The company invested significantly in trying to change key managers and directors, looking for younger people to implement changes in working practices. A few managers, however, saw this strategy to change culture from a different angle: they did not agree with the idea of 'replacing a massive number of managers'. Instead, they consider that 'managerial targets and outputs' must be changed. In other words, managers should be given a different framework. These managers believe that almost everyone can change his behaviour if given a chance. They also consider that by dismissing people, the company was losing important managers. As said by a Customer Services manager:

> We are losing people who have a lot of knowledge about our business and it is crucial.

Prevailing training and development Training development in BA aimed to be the lever for helping the organization to build a new corporate culture. Hence, the CEO decided to invest intensively in training the Customer Service Group. He focused primarily on the staff who deal directly with customers. Less than two months after taking charge, he said:

> We may need to put people through refresher courses to really concentrate on teaching staff how to sell the airline and its services (quoted from Bruce and Moult, 1988).

The immediate result was a series of seminars called 'Putting People First' (PPF) which was first held in November 1983. The key message was:

> If you feel ok about yourself you are more likely to feel ok about dealing with others.

Over two days the participants were treated to a mixture of presentations, exercises and group discussions.

> Staff were invited to review their personal experience of dealing with people in a broad way (at home, at work, etc.). They were introduced to concepts of setting personal goals and of taking responsibility for getting what they wanted out of life. There were confidence building exercises and an analysis of the power of expectation. The giving and receiving of attention was an important area of analysis ... Simple techniques of behavioural modification were also taught to help staff develop new approaches to dealing with upsets, coping with stress and developing a more positive attitude to themselves and others (Bruce and Moult, 1988).

These initiatives were aimed at the junior staff level, but there was an increasing recognition that a change in management style was needed.

> If they want staff to treat passengers as individuals, thus showing care and concern for passenger problems, then they have to do this to staff (Bruce, 1987).

There was an underlying dilemma: managers were asked to care for their people but they did not feel they were cared for at a personal level themselves.

Therefore, another course was designed as an attempt to fill this appointed mentioned gap. Under the Human Resource Director, Dr Nick Georgettes (appointed CEO in September 1984), a one week seminar was developed specifically for the 1,400 BA managers, entitled 'Managing People First' (MPF). Its specific aim was to implement the philosophy of 'emotional labour' by changing the historical impersonal culture into a culture which reinforced 'the business of caring and trust'. This type of approach was radically different from the 'cold, but fair' personnel philosophy in the past.

Although MPF had apparently the support of the CEO (as he attended eighty per cent of the meetings), senior line managers were not at all involved in its implementation. Besides, it appears also that the board of directors did not support this initiative. It seems that the HR department was responsible for the programme and, as a consequence, was perceived as imposing a strategy to change management style.

MPF was perceived by managers as disassociated from the changes occurring in other areas of the organization. For example, MPF was emphasizing 'trust' as an important new corporate value. However, as the philosophy of job security had been abolished, the issue of 'trust' became unclear for most managers.

> People now can lose jobs if something goes wrong ... We don't have security any more. Perhaps we are here only for today. Trust is based on security.

There are 'contradictions' in the messages managers are receiving during this transitional phase of the organization: The message of MPF was that it was important to have a 'warm' organization. However, in prevailing culture, managers interviewed felt the work place environment was 'warmer' before this process of culture change. This contradictory situation might reflect a 'clash' in values between different layers in the organization.

> Some people saw an inherent conflict between the values being promulgated by MPF and the reality of the management style in the workplace. They concluded that there is something more important than training to change managerial behaviour: top managers have to "model" the behaviour they want from staff (Bruce and Moult, 1988).

Managerial behaviour change implies first a modification in the 'role models'. This is reinforced by another manager's account:

> There is not a lot of point in taking water out of a muddy pool and purifying it, if all you are going to do is pour it back in the pool.

Another initiative coming from the Human Resource department is providing managers with MBA courses. Additionally, managers are moved around the organization in order to be exposed to different areas and therefore to widen their knowledge of the organization.

Some other training needs were identified in the process of change:

> The problem is, of course, to be a successful business man, you have to have some numerical ability. There are few people with this knowledge in the organization. Everybody is interested in talking, meetings, putting their views on how the culture should change. People need to be trained to read the numbers properly. The information comes from the data bases, and people do not know how to interpret them, how to analyse the data in order to be able to highlight what is most important to be focused on.

IT area has changed significantly its approach:

> We are now more open to developing ourselves. For example we are having a series of seminars on information technology which help us not only to talk with managers from other areas but also to discover what other companies and industries are doing regarding specific issues in information technology.

Prevailing managerial selection, appraisal, rewards Although many managers are trying to select new people utilizing the new criteria ('management skills'), some of them still prefer doing it in an old fashioned way, promoting and selecting people who are good technicians. The following two quotations emphasize the conflict between old and new values in the selection and promotion process:

> It is a disaster because if we choose a technician to be a manger, he dies like a plant if you don't water it.

> Managers are still being promoted under the old criteria. They are not coping well in this change process. They ignore the signals around them, they keep doing what they did in the past.

Although BA pays lip service to the concept of looking for a cultural fit, they are still struggling to find the right person for jobs, as seen by human resource staff.

> I am disappointed by how much recruitment has been biased by "people knowing people". The old boy network to a certain degree still works very strongly. It is probably because we do not have any faith in any other systems to identify potential at the moment. I do not think, consequently, that we are getting appropriate people for jobs. Many good people do not get the chance for jobs. They should get a chance. But just because they are unknown ... More attention should be given to this issue in order to avoid the usual mistakes we make.

In marketing areas, the criteria for choosing managers had changed from technical to management skills and abilities. They were looking for people who are able to implement changes and have the flexibility to work in different areas.

> We select people based on their personalities, managerial abilities rather than their experience because the world is changing so fast for us, experience is not necessarily an advantage. Because you would have been in companies where they use mindsets which

64

are no longer relevant. Experience is only valuable to help you to do things in the future. If the future is very different from the past, then, the experience is not valid at all. We prefer people with less experience than those carrying a "big bag".

Although BA has introduced, as a corporate initiative, a very sophisticated method for management appraisal, it has not worked as expected, each department appraises its people in a different way.

Performance related payment was introduced. Some areas however still reward managers according to the old values.

For example, they are still rewarding people based on their technical knowledge, instead of how they manage people.

The figure below shows the historical and the prevailing mission/culture/career systems at BA.

	Historical		Prevailing
Mission:	• to be a safe airline	**Mission:**	• to be a competitive airline • to be a safe airline
Culture:	• formality • bureaucracy • technical bias • authoritarian • safety	**Culture:**	• formality v informality • bureaucracy v innovation • technical bias v commercially oriented • participative v authoritarian
Careers:	• towards specialization (technical competence) • slow career (length in the service) • rewarding by seniority	**Careers:**	• customer oriented training (across functions) • participative management style training • performance related rewards • selection/promotion technical competence v management skills

Figure 8 Culture change and managerial careers: BA

The metaphor of BA culture as a personality

The 'old' BA personality

An ageing colonel, cold, introverted. I can see a picture of an old colonel sitting in his chair with his stick and not moving.

Very pudding like, very stuck in the mud, perhaps lethargic, apathetic in terms of how it was seen by the outside world.

Very slow, looking at details, conservative, not imaginative, never looking for new procedures, never asking staff for new work methods.

Completely formal, boring... It was stuffy, it was slow, like a bear, moving about slowly, ponderously, it was impersonal, there were a lot of rituals and things that you could not do. Much more awareness of status in the organization.

The 'new' BA personality

We are inconsistent. You cannot go to one part of the organization and know the whole. It all depends on where you are. It is still quite formal. There is a formality and an informality. It is structured and not structured. It is everything: old fashioned and modern. Again, it depends on where you are in the company.

For IT and sales managers, BA's personality is much more dynamic than it was before:

Fast moving ... flexible ... a sparkling personality, high profile, energetic.

A person who welcomes challenges, looking for new opportunities... this new person has a more positive approach to the working environment we are in today. Yesterday we were very negative.

Relatively very fast moving (not enough for the real world), more business oriented than before.

Managers from more technical areas do not feel that BA's personality has changed as was expected. One manager reported that the only noticeable change was:

We used to call people by surnames. Today we use their first names in all our internal documents. That is all I can tell you about changes in BA's personality.

British Airports Authority (BAA) case study

Introduction

Contrary to the three previous case studies, in this one BAA's managers reported that its culture had been an evolutionary one. This characteristic seems to reflect primarily the constantly growing industrial environment: the airports.

According to managers I interviewed, BAA was never a static organization. The company was seen as always being open to the outside world. However, the privatization process had sharpened its rhythm of change. Therefore, the values and beliefs of the organization had not been thoroughly challenged by managers, as was documented in the previous three case studies. Hence, traits of BAA organizational culture (both historical and prevailing) seemed to remain taken for granted and difficult to uncover. Consequently, the data sometimes look superficial as they relate mainly to management behaviour and attitudes rather than to the organizational values and beliefs. It seemed that BAA managers always considered their corporate culture a successful one.

A briefing of the company (from various annual reports)

BAA's core business is the ownership and operation of airports. Through its subsidiaries at Heathrow, Gatwick, Stansted, Glasgow, Edinburgh, Prestwick and Aberdeen it handles seventy percent of UK passenger traffic and eighty five per cent of air cargo.

Since flotation on The Stock Exchange in July 1987, BAA has expanded into areas complementary to the core airport business; these include property development, hotels, flight and international airport operations.

BAA is unique in being a publicly owned international airport company. Heathrow and Gatwick maintain their position as the world's first and second busiest international airports.

In 1989 BAA employed 8,000 people in the UK, 3,600 of whom are located at Heathrow. BAA enjoys the privileged position of a monopoly within and around London. However, the focus of competitive rivalry is not domestic but international; principally from Amsterdam, Frankfurt and Paris.

Methodology

In BAA, the data collection took place just two years after its privatization. Some managers considered that it was too early to look back and reflect on the impact of specific changes on the organization as a whole. One manager's opinion was:

> It seems to me a fascinating subject, the links between careers and culture change - they really exist. However, only two years after privatization it is still a bit early to look back and make judgements. I think we need at least five years, then there would be a historical perspective. The further we go, we can understand better the process of change. I think that all the accelerated changes which came with privatization have been good for the organization. But we are still on the track... we shall see...

Data was collected from middle and mainly senior managers across the organization. Seventeen interviews altogether were conducted during July/August 1989. Five managers were from human resource areas, twelve from other areas in different subsidiaries. The sample was chosen by the person who was my contact in the organization - 'the key informant' (Human Resources senior manager).

As a result of managers' perceptions, the process of culture change in BAA can be analysed in two distinct periods:

1 'Historical', from 1966 (its creation) to 1975, the appointment of a new Managing Director - MD

2 'Prevailing'
  a) 1976 to 1985 - pre privatization period
  b) 1985 to 1989 - privatization period

As shown above, the periods of investigation in BAA are slightly different from those of the previous case studies. That is, the historical period characterized by bureaucracy lasted from the creation of the company until 1975, when the new MD and Chairman started to reshape the old civil service culture. When I asked interviewees to explain the management behaviour *before* and *after* privatization, they all reacted in a very interesting way as shown in the following quotation:

> ... There is no *before* and *after*. We have been experiencing an evolution process in our cultures and also in our human resource practices since 1976.

Coincidentally, the appointment of a MD (1975) was identified by managers as the beginning of a faster moving organization. This MD was described by all managers as someone who brought many new ideas to manage the company. Similarly, the appointment of a CEO, in 1985, has launched another cultural era. This data confirms Schein's (1983a) and Watson's (1963) ideas on a leader's values and their impact on organizational culture.

BAA's history

BAA was created in 1966 as a result of the existing government process of nationalization. Prior to the creation of BAA, various government departments were responsible for the operation of the UK airports. Therefore, BAA employees generally possessed a civil service background. In the past, managers perceived themselves as not 'that strongly led by profits'... more paternalistic, i.e. 'concentrating on the welfare of the employees'.

The majority of managers interviewed had been employed by BAA for over twenty years. One of them describes her perceptions of people's behaviour in the past as:

> Civil service... It gives you a whole scenario of how people behave, what they were expected to do, how much freedom, how much initiative, and how much thinking was required of them. Everything was run by rules; there was a tendency to look backwards to make sure that you were absolutely fair to everybody under all circumstances.

As a reflection of the mainly civil service type of culture, BAA's structure was highly centralized. Consequently, most decisions were made by the 'heavy head office'. Managers didn't have to make decisions about their staff. This is illustrated by the quotation:

> For example, if someone came to me saying: "my grandmother died yesterday. I would like to go to the funeral on Friday". I, as a manager could not decide about this issue. Personnel people would analyse the situation and make the decision they found appropriate. It was not right. I, as a manager, should analyse the situation and decide according to my previous knowledge of that individual.

Analysis of the corporate culture

This section is divided into two periods:

a)   'historical' culture - 1966 to 1975
b)   'prevailing' culture - 1976 to 1989

BAA 'historical' culture 1966 to 1975

This section explores managers' perceptions on the organizations main values and of the management style required in the past. It is a retrospective analysis covering the period between 1966, its creation, and 1975 when a MD was appointed.

a) The historical 'core mission' Both the data collected via managers and official documentation show that BAA's core mission (contrary to Jaguar, BNFL and BA) had always reflected a commercial orientation. A manager comments: 'We aimed to give good service but also to make some profits'.
The Annual Report (1966) defines the mission of the organization thus:

> ... an efficient commercial enterprise dedicated to the task of providing at its airports worthy gateways to Britain... To promote a sound financial policy... While concentrating upon steadily improving service to the travelling public, the cargo shippers, the airline and all other users of its airports (p. 3).

According to managers, commercial awareness stemmed from the nature of BAA's core business. In other words, there has always been an emphasis placed on the development of associated 'value added' services to complement the core airport business.

> Our culture grew commercial because we always had a duty free operation. We were providing retailing and catering opportunities... in some instances we provided the necessary investment in facilities (shops) and, in return, we retained a share of either the profits or the income.

Another manager's account reinforces this idea of a commercial culture:

> In the past ten years we have been aware of value for money, we never saw ourselves as a drain on resources from the government. On the contrary, we were contributing.

b) 'Historical' management style Managers in the past believed that, as a consequence of position and status in the organization, the staff would respond to them. This is reinforced by the quotation:

> ... because there was a very rigid hierarchy, it was not that important which kind of style you adopted.

There is a consensus among managers that, historically, the company employed generalists in the majority of the key positions rather than specialist managers. This perception can be confirmed by two managers' accounts:

> I describe myself as a generalist. I had to develop a degree of knowledge about catering, commercial and public relations. I relied on my colleagues who were specialists (personnel, finance or engineering) to help me in managing other areas.

It was also clear from data analysis that managers perceived the day to day working practices of the past as slower than those of the last few years.

> It was better to get it 100 per cent right even if that took a long time to do... perhaps it was not such a crime, things take a long time to do.

As seen by the interviewees, this type of slow response, however, has been modified over the years as a consequence both of new demands from the growing industry and of the type of people being recruited. They see themselves as becoming gradually more open to environmental demands as a way to survive in this type of industry.

BAA 'prevailing' culture 1976 to 1989

a) 1976 to 1985 - pre privatization period
b) 1985 to 1989 - privatization period

The prevailing culture in BAA is studied in two periods: before and during privatization. As explained earlier, in 1976 a MD was appointed and gradually changes in working practices started to occur. In 1985 (beginning of the privatization period), a CEO was appointed and drastically introduced some changes in the organization, reshaping the organizational culture.

a) Pre privatization period - 1976 to 1985 Following the appointment of new MD in 1976, managers would always be encouraged to present new ideas to higher levels of the organization. As a consequence of my pursuing this issue, a senior manager reported his views emphasizing the top management values.

> We were always an adventurous company. The chairman was always open to new ideas. The MD and the directors were then responsible for presenting him with new strategies to be implemented.

Also as a result of in depth discussion with interviewees, one manager emphasized another reason for the innovative and open culture which is the type of industry BAA is in.

> We do not produce anything, we provide services, we need to be able to react to the needs of our customers. Mainly the passengers and the airline. The airline has very significant demands which are always changing: new aircraft coming, bigger aircraft, noisy, with higher wings, low wings... You have to be prepared to be flexible. And yet, because it is so expensive to run an airport, it has to be one which will last a long time as well, which requires being adaptable, being open.

Data revealed that BAA is concerned about the role of communication. This could also be seen in the way I was treated as a researcher in BAA, compared to other organizations. At Jaguar, they tried to present a sophisticated image; BNFL, as I experienced it, was secretive and reserved, despite the sincerity of the interviewees' contacts; BA was very formal, reserved, and somewhat untrusting of my role as researcher. In BAA, however, I felt like a welcome customer since friendly communication, trust and correspondence were the predominant tone throughout the interviews. This is also supported by a manager's account:

71

> The company is very keen on improving staff relations, and to do a better job in terms of communications, cascading information down to staff. We do not have quality circles as such, but we try to work on that sort of basis. We try to communicate to staff at all levels, in other words, we try to get the morale up.

Evidence which corroborates this interpretation is seen in the way some managers described the pre privatization decision making process.

> Before 1985, there was an executive committee run by the MD, where all the directors of central functions - Finance, Engineering, Airports - sat together and made the decisions. The MD was trying to get a consensus... He listened to everybody and made the decision. It was his decision, after considering everybody's point of view.

It seems to me that, since 1976, BAA has been run with a management style where two way communication has always been encouraged, however, the final decision was always left to the MD.

b) Privatization period - 1985 to 1989 - the new core mission It was clearly a decision taken by the Chairman, prior to privatization, that the company would have a CEO who would introduce a financial mindset which would be welcomed by the City. In the same way, when they were a nationalized industry, the chairman put a lot of effort into establishing a proper relationship with the government. 'He was very conscious of this new need'.

Pressures from share holders and city financial institutions have led to a greater emphasis on the ancillary businesses such as hotels and catering which are deemed to offer a higher rate of return. This re-orientation can be attributed to the new CEO's financial background. This measure, however, was not well accepted by managers, who considered it would be against their successful historical culture. A senior manager says:

> Eighty five per cent of our activities are airports (and still growing rapidly). The CEO was placing most of his energy and time in the other fifteen per cent of other business activities... it was concerning the Executive board... if we continued until the end of the century, the business would be going down hill...

A middle manager's account emphasizes the strong culture within BAA:

> We are good at managing airports... the skills required to run airports are the things we are unique and good at... because no one else in the UK has those skills, we have tried to develop managers in managing airports and we need to keep that. We can sell our experience overseas. We are not as good in doing other activities or we have no experience of other things!

I found a contradiction in management responses regarding the perception of the organization's new mission. Although managers tend to deny that privatization has brought any drastic changes, at the same time, the data revealed that people suffered a 'cultural shock' when the new mission was established by the CEO.

72

Ten years ago the main idea was to give good service with high quality, safety and security and to do that at a reasonable cost. Not to be extravagant, not to waste money, but on the other hand not too concerned about every pound used. The majority of people felt that it is not immoral making profits, but that it should be done in a more considered way. They were shocked by the statement '100 per cent profits' imposed by the new CEO.

Although BAA has always been a commercially oriented organization, the emphasis on the financial aspects of the business became more relevant after privatization, according to the managers. The following account illustrates this interpretation.

The use of the word 'profits' was not very common. It was not in the front of people's minds. After privatization, the word 'profits' became a more common feature for people, and people's pay became more linked to profits.

The new management structure/style Privatization instigated changes in the organization's structure. Each airport was set up as its own limited company, with profit centres, producing their own financial results. This gave a great degree of independence to each of these companies. This is in great contrast to the old structure where the head office dictated policy to the individual airports. Instead, they have created a small corporate office, close to the city of London. The responsibility and the budget control was delegated to each subsidiary.

Everything now is much more immediate, we can control what we want to do at a much more local level without having to refer to the centre. As each airport is a limited company, it has to solve its own problems locally... This large centralized personnel department was pulled apart, dismantled, and pushed down to the subsidiary companies.

Human resources is now a service to line managers. It is reversing the role... 'A huge transformation'. Gradually, the personnel department's power has been devolving. This movement started around six years ago, and was accelerated by privatization. 'It was made overnight'. There is no longer a Personnel Director in BAA. They have a saying:

Managers must manage their own people, not Personnel.

In order to fit in this new structure, managers need a much broader view of the business, a 'more complete manager'. Managers see themselves under pressure to be more fast moving.

What is happening now is, we require a style of management which achieves things in a much shorter period of time. Some of the timescales we achieve now, in the past, you would have said it is impossible. Now, whether or not we cross every 't' and dot every 'i' in the process, the fine details, getting all the words absolutely right, it is not now the question. But, again, if we achieve the end objectives by introducing this or that, that is how we are judged now.

73

As a consequence of the new mission plan and structure, the style of management and the expected behaviour has been adjusted accordingly. Managers are more business orientated and financially aware and given greater individual freedom to operate their particular airports on an individual basis. The centrally controlled/planned nature of the business, traditionally associated with its civil service origins, has disappeared.

In the past, if you had a problem with your money, financial departments would deal with it; your staff problems, Personnel would deal with.

The turnaround in what was expected from managers was 'absolutely incredible'.

... We realise now that there is more scope for us to do things and do things differently. Managers are more business conscious, certainly more financially aware with more emphasis on costs than there was when I first joined the organization ten years ago.

Although most of the decisions have been more delegated to the companies, financial issues, the decision making process regarding finance has become more bureaucratic, 'many controls were introduced'.

We gain some freedom, also some additional controls.

Q: Is there any link between CEO/founder's style and the management style as a whole?

A: Yes. It is inevitable.

The above dialogue, extracted from my original tape transcriptions, matches with what Schein (1985a) says:

Managers, in a sense, impose their own style on the organizational life (p. 75).

In order to investigate the relationship between the leaders' values and culture, I asked questions relating to perceptions of the management style of the chairman (working in BAA from 1963 to present); the MD (working in BAA from 1965 to 1985), and the CEO (working in BAA from 1985 to 1989). Managers described top management values in a positive way:

Although our origins lie in the public sector, we had people at the top, particularly in the 1970s, who wanted to run this company as a business not just as a public utility. So, to some extent we were fortunate, in my view.

The Chairman is open. He listens to people, goes out into the organization and sees people.

From approximately 1975 to 1985, two top managers were running BAA. The Chairman (a fairly "strong" style) and the MD, who came from industry, was "highly participative" (his emphasis), with a very open management style. He was highly respected, out and about in the business, going places, seeing people, talking with people, talking to people on the shop floor. The MD and Chairman made a good team. The Chairman was looking to the business, the policies. The Chairman and MD worked as a balanced team: one very strong, one very smooth. The result was very good. The

74

MD was the gear box, converting the energy and power of the Chairman, controlling and applying his energy.

As perceived by managers, both the Chairman and the ex MD hold values which encouraged two way communication and a participative style of management. They were seen to be looking at the terminals, looking into things. The company has had the same Chairman all the way through. He exemplifies a very analytical type of management, as seen by managers, reflecting his engineering background. He has a 'high profile', he is described as a 'visible manager' (Peters and Waterman, 1982).

The new CEO (from 1985 to 1989), however, practised a totally different management style from the MD. His style derived perhaps, from his background as an accountant. He was 'very autocratic', with a 'totally closed management style'. 'It didn't work'. 'Low profile', he was interested in the 'bottom line profitability of the business' and essentially concerned with the bottom line results.

The contrasting styles of the Chairman and CEO had an impact on the way the organization was run.

> The impression we had from our CEO (perhaps also due to his background experience), that he was trying to push this organization for short term thinking and acting (you had to think on next month, next year) instead of long term.

This conflict situation in organizational culture was clearly reported, in a consensus, by all senior managers interviewed. As perceived by interviewees, the top management's new strategy of dealing with people within the organization was seen by the people as a whole, as 'killing or destroying the well established corporate culture'. These values and beliefs had been reinforced both by past leaders' 'role models' (Chairman and MD) and by the success of the company so far (as reported by interviewees and also annual reports). This conflict reduced the morale of employees and also affected productivity. As one manager said:

> When you receive different guidance from the top, then the managers become confused regarding their priorities.

This management conflict, however, is better expressed by the following quotation:

> Directors and managers tend to try to mirror who they perceive is running the organization. Otherwise they don't stay, do they?

This CEO had left the company just before the interviews took place. A few managers reported that he resigned, many others, though, reported that he was dismissed as he did not fit into the BAA culture.

Analysis of the managerial careers

This section is devoted to the analysis of how BAA has been managing careers for managers. Following the same pattern as in the other case studies, it covers two distinct phases: The 'historical' (1966 to 1975) and the 'prevailing' (1976 to 1989).

The 'historical' managerial careers

Traditionally, personnel functions were centralized and managers were almost 'hiding behind Personnel'. They had, in the past, a 'very dominant' Personnel Department. Hence, recruitment decisions were made centrally.

a) 'Historical' recruitment and selection As perceived by the interviewees, the recruitment and selection systems impinged in a very significant way on the process of culture change in BAA. Different people coming in had reshaped its culture.

> This is my experience during the first ten years I worked here - 1968 to 1978: In the beginning practically everybody was a civil servant. Over that ten year period, a lot of other people came from outside. So it was a gradual process of changing people. At the end of the ten years, BAA was an entirely different organization. It was more innovative, more commercial. But changes have occurred gradually, almost imperceptibly. Only at the end of these years, looking back, we can see that it has changed. But it was not the same kind of change which came with privatization. The later one was more drastic.

Instead of a uniform managerial profile throughout the company, BAA managers revealed a great awareness of the need for managerial profile to reflect sub cultures within the company. They need people with two types of skills, i.e. planning skill (such as 'thinking ahead') and immediate skills ('able to solve immediate problems'). A senior manager said:

> The nature of the business requires managers to take a lot of instant decisions, if an airplane needs to land suddenly, we have to be quick, to be immediate. A lot of managers live in a world of immediacy. So managers get a lot of points for action. We also need people who think in the future, the planning people... we know that to build a terminal we need ten years.

b) 'Historical' promotion Managerial promotion, in the past, was much slower than now. There were many different bureaucratic criteria to be met if managers wanted to get up the career ladder. *Length in the job and age* were the most weighty criteria.

> Indeed, in my first promotion opportunity, I was not allowed to apply because of my age. I could not get that level of job until I was twenty one. All that has gone now...

76

In the past, every single job in the company had to be advertised company wide. There was a three man interview board, and 'too many procedures'.

> I do not think that ten years ago someone of my age would have been necessarily expected to do this sort of job within the organization. Several of my peers, certainly three out of the other four, are in their early 30s. Now the managers are younger, using a more modern approach. Some of the old managers became bypassed in the process. Either they retired or other managers came on top of them. When we have this kind of mix, the culture spreads out by itself.

Apart from administrative rules (such as age and length in the job), the performance criteria also differ from the past. Different requirements were then used to promote managers. For instance, stress tolerance and persuasiveness were not important traits in the past. A manager explained why.

> We did not have high levels of industrial security. When I started to work at Gatwick, we were dealing with four million passengers a year, now it is twenty one million.

c) 'Historical' training and development In the past, managers in BAA were 'made', not trained. The best technician would be promoted to be a supervisor or manager. Afterwards, he would be sent to some kind of training, usually general courses. Hence, in the past, managers were not prepared for the jobs.

Gradually, the emphasis on training and developing, as a way to prepare managers before actually taking charge, increased. It is interesting to note that interviewees themselves make the links between top management values and managerial career systems.

> In Gatwick our emphasis on training can be explained as a reflection of the MD, an ex personnel manager.

d) 'Historical' appraisal and performance In the past, BAA's appraisal of performance was quite separate from salary.

> In the past, the appraisal system was more loose. There were budgets, objectives to be achieved, but they were not pay related

The annual appraisal included no discussion regarding salaries.

> It changed very gradually, but not as much as it has changed during the last ten years.

During the process of interviewing managers in BAA, the issue of change was always mentioned by them even when talking about historical culture or historical career systems.

For the purpose of the analysis of 'prevailing' managerial careers, I will integrate the two phases - before and during privatization - since they appear very similar to each other. However, when differences occur, these will be indicated in the text.

Differing from BNFL and BA, where both culture and careers seemed more static before privatization, BAA has been changing its culture and human resource practices over the past fourteen years, i.e. since 1976 when the MD was appointed. Consequently, managers cannot identify any major changes in career systems between these two phases, except the emphasis on financial skills which occurred during the privatization period.

Although interviewees admit that privatization has accelerated the process of change in the organization, for some managers the real motives for such changes are related to the turbulent environment.

> I do not think that privatization is the only reason to explain our modifications in our way of doing things. In fact, there is a gradual change in the nature of the business: for instance, the political arena we are operating in, the Conservative party, the labour market situation.

a) *'Prevailing' recruitment and selection* Since 1976, managerial recruitment has been one of the main changes in personnel practices. Because of the expansion of the airport business, and also because a private organization requires 'an injection of expertise', BAA do not have the necessary managers to fill up all posts. Therefore, they are now using external advertising as well as being 'more critical' in hiring people.

> We are looking more critically at managers for the future - the 1990s.

In the last couple of years, the company has changed four out of seven members of the board. 'Only one of these replacements didn't work, the CEO,' said one of the Human Resource Managers. According to managers' perceptions, it is fundamental, during this process of culture change, that top management is an integrated team.

> We need a balanced team at the top, the right group mix. The dynamics of the team at the top is crucial. If they do not interact well, it is a trouble.

BAA is now using 'criteria interview method' to select managers. It is more specific than it was in the past.

Criteria for selecting managers BAA is now more concerned than it was in the past about management selection and promotion.

> We are now more critical in identifying who gets selected and promoted.

78

There is a consensus that the 'participative' style of management is one criterion being used to select managers since 1976 when MD was appointed.

> In the early days of BAA, there was a rigid hierarchy and the style of leadership that managers adopted was not relevant. Then gradually, a great need for leaders to understand about involving the work force, has emerged. Participative style became very important.

There is also a consensus that 'team work' has been necessary to accomplish the tasks.

> Because changes in the business are much faster, there is a *realisation* that no one person can do it on his own. The only way to get things done in a service organization is through the people you employ. We are so dependent on people on the line that team work is vital, you cannot operate in isolation, you have to relate well with peers.

'Analytical skills', 'adaptability' and 'openness' are considered very important for all levels of management in BAA. Again, this seems to reflect the Chairman's own profile. He has been described by managers as 'having a very analytical personality'.

A manager explains why the managerial style today is different from the past:

> Because the world does not stay still, we need good decision makers and hard workers... because, in the old days, the rhythm of work was slower, there was not much pressure. Now, without commitment to hard work you cannot survive in the organization. We want people who can manage change, who are not frightened by new ventures or new concepts, who have skills to take the work force with them, also to understand the importance of training because the organization has given a lot of emphasis to training.

Managers in BAA seem to be aware that these management profile is unique to each kind of organizational culture.

> If you go to another organization you will have a different order of criteria for managerial requirements. It must be a product of *internal search* (his emphasis).

b) 'Prevailing' promotion Historically, there was an element of chance in whether somebody was successful or not. People are now being promoted according to their performance. This is illustrated by the following quotation:

> For example, in the past, because my boss was retiring and I was his assistant, I would automatically get the job. Today, this job could be filled by someone from other departments, maybe this person has been working in this company for only a short period of time. If we think he is the chap, he will get the job.

The company is becoming more systematic about its own needs, and also matching people and jobs more accurately.

> We need to have a clear idea of a manager's potential and also the requirements for a specific job.

The privatization process forced the organization to become more financially oriented. Before privatization, it was possible for managers to come up in the organization without really having any financial awareness. Today, they cannot do a job, at a senior level, unless they have that financial understanding.

BAA is now looking for people who can manage change:

> We need people who know what to do when tomorrow is different from yesterday, and the day after will be different again. People who can cope with various different pressures, know what sort of information they want in order to be able to cope with change.

To summarize the necessary profile for a BAA manager: There are some competences that the managers have to have: finance, IT, marketing. As individuals, they have to know how to build a team, and how to develop its members personally as well. Managers are being promoted under a wider range of criteria: financial skills, personnel skills, 'a much broader range of skills than historically'.

BAA seems to be aware of the different sub cultures within the organization. To fit these sub cultures, different management profiles are necessary, as explained by a manager.

> Taking two streams, we need two different kinds of manager. One job is running an airport, the other is heading the planning sector at corporate level. For the latter, we need the academics, the theorists. In a financial or engineering sector, we need a totally different person. It is important to get the right fit.

For example, the criteria BAA use to select candidates to be an airport manager are: flexibility, stress tolerance, participative style, leadership, adaptability, persuasiveness, problem analysis, judgment, decisiveness, management control and delegation. They consider that 'adaptability' is a characteristic necessary for many different jobs in BAA.

c) *'Prevailing' training and development* It is noticeable that managers feel proud when talking about their human resource practices, mainly their training and development activities.

> We consider ourselves a very advanced company regarding management development.

The managerial training needs have changed in response to different management requirements. In the past, for example, they used to train people in 'how to perform their own jobs'. Now they are trying to make them aware of the help they can receive from other staff areas, for example, the benefits of information technology.

> Many senior managers grew up in a pre computer era, they are not really aware of the sort of information they can have and the effects of this in the decision making process.

The training philosophy at BAA during the process of culture change has not been based on changing people's values in a direct way via behavioural workshops. They aim to equip people with the skills they need to do the job in a changing environment. One thing they have identified is the need for finance training and budget experience. Managers now have to understand the impact of costs on the business. As the core values shift from an emphasis on service to an emphasis on finance, training activities reflect this. The emphasis on finance seems to stem from the new corporate mission recently established by the Chairman and CEO. Although rarely explicitly stated, the concept 'corporate culture' is present in BAA managers' thinking. They realise how unique BAA is as an entity with its particularities, therefore, they value 'in house' training and development. It can be illustrated by the comment:

> We cannot buy managers from elsewhere because there are no other organizations doing the same thing. For example, if a chemical company has a shortage of chemical managers, then they hire some chemists from elsewhere...

Another manager's account reinforces this idea:

> Running an airport is like running a small town. Everything you visualise in a town is actually in an airport. It is not easy. You can't go outside and just recruit managers because they are not there.

In order to make sure that the managers were equipped to handle their own problems, much effort went into:

1   Training managers, and

2   Giving them responsibility for matters that previously belonged to personnel or finance department.

Currently managers are responsible for running their own human resource systems. However, they can still come to personnel for advice. 'It seems to be a more healthy relationship'.

In the assessment centres, line managers with the support of personnel managers (who act as facilitators), try to highlight weaknesses in managers that can be improved, for example, 'stress tolerance' or 'management control'. A lack of these characteristics can be identified in order to give the appropriate direction to the manager's development, as perceived by managers I interviewed.

> Assessment centres are certainly good ways to identify training needs.

Although BAA also uses external consultants to train their staff, managers or experts from BAA are invited to participate in the training sections as tutors. They use case studies as a method to explore real situations. This training strategy seems to reinforce the organizational culture. As tutors, managers

81

can present their own ideas of how to handle specific situations on a day to day basis in BAA.

BAA tend to identify people's potential earlier. With graduates this is easy. With senior managers, however, they consider that it is more complex.

d) 'Prevailing' reward and appraisal system In BAA, the appraisal system is one of the sources of management development. It is used for changing jobs even if it does not involve an increase in salary.

BAA, over the last eight years, has implemented a new appraisal system. In this new system, managers are assessed on performance against targets. Their strengths and weaknesses, as managers, are evaluated and the potential for progress identified. There is a feedback process. It ensures that the manager and the subordinates know what the subordinate is supposed to be doing. The performance related appraisal system was introduced by the chairman.

> The chairman was the first chairman of a nationalized industry who had his own pay related to his performance. He wanted to be judged by performance. The chairman has been supporting the idea of performance related pay for many years.

Since privatization, however, a significant part of a senior manager's pay has become profit related. This has happened in two ways: i) pay is determined by a figure for the following year, based on current performance; ii) each subsidiary wins bonuses to senior executives for its profitability, and for achieving key targets in areas such as finance, services, project management.

Discussion

As clarified in this case study, BAA's corporate culture was formed as a product of the airport service industry's values (commercially biased) and the founder's values (openness flexibility). The process of culture change in BAA differs mainly from the previous case studies regarding its intensity/pace. It means BAA's culture has always been characterized as 'innovative' and receptive to environmental change.

As an evolutionary process, both culture and careers have been modified in response to environmental demands over the years. In the preparation for privatization, however, a more accelerated process of change occurred. The organization's core mission has changed to emphasize profits rather than services. Radical changes took place in the organizational structure (decentralisation). As a consequence, managers' responsibilities have increased.

As mentioned above, privatization did not instigate the process of change in BAA but accelerated it. The company was never seen as static.

This constant process of gradual change is explained by managers as being linked to two reasons:

1   the dynamism which characterizes the airport industry and also its growing process.

2   the Chairman and ex MD's management profile.

As shown in figure 9, features of the culture before and during privatization periods are similar. For instance, BAA both in the past (after 1976) and currently value flexibility, innovation, openness and participative management style.

	Pre privatization		Post privatization
Mission:	• provide good service • be profitable	**Mission:**	• be profitable • provide good service
Culture:	• commercially biased • flexibility • innovation • openness	**Culture:**	• financially oriented • flexibility • innovation • openness
Careers:	• towards generalists • participative style of management • teamwork • communication skills	**Careers:**	• towards general expertise • financial skills (budgeting) • personnel management skills • participative style • teamwork • communication skills

Figure 9 Culture change and managerial careers: BAA

Few features of the organization, however, differentiate when we compare these two periods. For example, financial skills are more valued at BAA currently than they were before privatization. This can be observed not only from the day to day statements, but by the way careers are managed. For example, in training, much attention has been given to teaching managers about budget and other necessary financial tools. In selection and promotion, financial skills have now become more relevant than before. Appraisal and reward systems are now, at least partially, based on the level of profitability achieved by managers.

A unique characteristic of BAA culture, as compared to the previous studies, is that BAA has always been managed by generalists. Diversification away from the core business, and the acceleration in the rate of industry and organizational growth have only re-emphasized their need for generalists. For example, as a consequence of the decentralisation of the personnel area, managers are expected to deal with personnel issues which in the past were delegated to the HQ.

Conclusions

Following the patterns of previous case studies, after privatization, the mission, culture and careers systems have been modified. In this case, they have changed from a service oriented to a profit oriented mission/culture.

An unexpected result coming from this case study is that privatization did not instigate changes in BAA, but just accelerated them. Culture change in BAA was a result of a growing industry and identifying with top management values. Similarly, commercial awareness did not come with privatization, but as part of a commercially biased industry.

As in BNFL and unlike Jaguar and BA, managers in BAA seem to be aware that different sub cultures require different managerial profiles. However, some core values are constant and seem to be consistent throughout the organization: innovation, communication, flexibility and adaptability.

Perhaps the most important issue that this case study can teach us about culture change process is that BAA has never tried to change people's values, but to change those of the company. In other words, efforts have been made to give managers different responsibilities as the business evolved.

Human resources' main objectives have been, over the years, to try to equip managers (via specific training) with the necessary management tools for them to act according to the changeable environmental demands. BAA's top management do not believe that new managers necessarily need to be selected from outside. BAA's human resource philosophy lies in the idea of providing managers with a wider view of the business because they believe that most managers can change their own behaviour.

6 UK cross case analysis: Jaguar Cars, BNFL, BA and BAA

Introduction

This chapter compares and contrasts the results of the four British case studies. Although each individual study (see Chapter 5), in isolation, tells an interesting and different story about the process of corporate culture change associated with privatization, it is useful to discuss the similarities and the most significant differences I found between them. Therefore, a cross case analysis method was chosen to analyse the four case studies under investigation. In this method, the entire explanation for each case is taken and compared with the explanation from another case. To the extent that the explanations are similar, the basis for a more general explanation can be established.

How culture was created in Jaguar, BNFL, BA and BAA

This research indicates that two major factors seem to be responsible for the process of creating corporate culture. These factors are:

1   Top leaders' values, and
2   The industry's dominant values.

The differences in these factors probably account for the different ways managers are expected to behave in these four organizations. Figure 10 displays the summary of findings of how culture was formed in Jaguar, BNFL, BA and BAA.

1 Top leaders' values: Historically, top management's values in these four companies varied enormously (see figure 10). It is amazing how much influence the founder and top leaders had on shaping the historical cultures. As Schein (1985b) observed, variations in style among top management arise because people grow up in different cultures, which make very different assumptions about the nature of the universe, truth, human nature and human relationships. Individuals initially vary in the cognitive assumptions they bring to a new group situation, and attempt to establish common frames of reference. This process, according to Schein (1985b), is clearly central to understanding cultural origins within a group.

Both Jaguar and BAA have always had a charismatic leader, although these have varied in their individual styles. Jaguar's founder was described by managers as an 'authoritarian, charismatic' leader (a view supported by the press). He believed in formality and distance between employees and managers and the expected managerial behaviour established by the founder as a way to 'get on' in Jaguar meant working in a dynamic way and working long hours. BAA also has a charismatic leader (the Chairman) who has remained in his post from the creation of the organization until the present day. As with Jaguar, the values of BAA's charismatic leader were reflected in the way managers were expected to behave. However, the founder's values in BAA seem to be completely different from those in Jaguar since he is described as prizing openness, flexibility and innovation and having a very analytical mind.

It is observed that BNFL and BA did not have such charismatic leaders as BAA and Jaguar. Consequently, each department reflected its own senior executive's values and beliefs.

2 The industry's dominant values: As Thackray (1986) observed, scarcely any literature exists on the influence of an industrial sector's specific values upon corporate culture. However, the results of this current study imply that this relationship is very important and raises issues for future research as identified in the concluding chapter.

As Gordon (1985) emphasises, different industries develop different cultural patterns to suit their business demands. For example, the film industry is miles apart culturally from banking; likewise the garment industry from automobile manufacture. These cultural patterns mentioned by Gordon (1985) are noticeable when comparing and contrasting the industry's dominant values between Jaguar, BNFL, BA and BAA. A description of each of these companies' principal activities is provided below. This is useful to identify their differences and the links between their culture and the industry's specific characteristics.

86

	Top leader's values	Industry's values	Historical expected managerial behaviour
Jaguar	**Charismatic founder** • Sophistication • Formality • Authoritarian • Enthusiasm (restless) • Drive, dynamism	**Luxury manufactured car** • High profile • Engineering biased • Individualism	• Formal • Dynamic/restless • Enthusiastic • Hard worker • Technical competent (Eng) • Work in isolation
BNFL	**Senior management** • Bureaucracy • Paternalism • Benevolence	**Nuclear Industry** • Perfectionism • Safety • Secrecy • Technical biased	• Obey the system • Perfectionist-specialist • 'A good chap'
BA	**Senior management values** • Bureaucracy • Military, regimented • Formality • Political	**Airline** • Security • Engineering biased	• Formal/regimented • Technically competent • Specialist
BAA	**Charismatic founder** • Informality • Creativity • Innovation • Openness	**Airports management** • Commercial biased • Customer oriented	• Commercial awareness • Participative • Openness-customer oriented • Generalistic

Figure 10   How culture was formed in Jaguar, BNFL, BA and BAA

87

- Jaguar is engaged in the design, development, manufacture and marketing of high performance luxury saloon cars and is a specialist in sports car production.

- BNFL's main activity is the production of nuclear fuels for the UK and overseas. Sellafield is the repository of the bulk of Britain's nuclear waste in terms of radioactivity. A characteristic of BNFL is the long lead time between order and delivery, anything from four to ten years.

- BA's principal activities are the operation of international and domestic scheduled and charter air services for the carriage of passengers and cargo. The airline provides other services such as the maintenance of aircraft and engine as well as passenger and cargo handling.

- BAA's principal business is the ownership and operation of seven international airports in the UK. Most of BAA's commercial revenues are derived from concessions, although a proportion comes from the renting to airlines, and others, of land and property for handling cargo and baggage as well as hotels and offices. Additionally, BAA provides the capital expenditure for car parks, restaurants and shops.

Jaguar and BNFL are manufacturing industries, whilst BA and BAA provide services. Although Jaguar and BNFL are manufacturers, they seem to possess opposite values, as a consequence of differences in type of product, technology and consumers. These differences are highlighted below:

BNFL, probably as a reflection of the nuclear industry, shows a very secretive type of culture which is reflected in the behaviour of all managers, and illustrated by managers' accounts of 'the need to know philosophy'. This is indicated by the fact that the majority of interviews were not conducted in the managers' offices, but in impersonal conference facilities or hotels, physically removed from the actual industrial location. Furthermore, the long lead time necessary to construct a power plant is reflected in the slow evolution of managerial practices. As one manager commented, 'It would be easier for us to change if we made dishwashers instead' - a competitive, high technology, consumer durable product.

Jaguar, by contrast, as a luxury car manufacturer, valued sophistication and dynamism whilst maintaining a high public profile. 'Managers want to be seen in public affairs'. During the field work, a chauffeur driven car was always available to take me from site to site - reinforcing the image of sophistication.

Unlike BNFL, all interviews were conducted in the managers' offices, and all show rooms were open to public inspection.

Although both BA and BAA belong to the service industry, they present contrasting historical cultures. BA managers considered themselves to be primarily engineering based, and their main aim was to keep their airplanes flying in excellent condition. Security and accuracy were described as being the main organizational values. They did not value being a profitable organization, but rather being a reliable airline.

In contrast, BAA have always had commercial awareness as part of their beliefs, stemming from their main activity of being landlords and, 'always having to make a profit out of the shops'. Selling has been part of their business since its creation.

The process of culture change in Jaguar, BNFL, BA and BAA

Although the process by which culture was created was similar in the four companies under study, the way culture transformed, varied enormously. The differences found in the process of culture 'change' seem to be a consequence of each CEO's leadership style and consequently of the strategy utilised to implement such changes. Although all the firms seemed to have been struggling in their transitional periods of change, this process appears to have been less painful in some than in others.

The need for change

This book analyses what took place regarding culture and managerial careers in four organizations during privatization. These were British organizations and each was having to cope with two major external new demands:

- change in ownership (from government owned to public).
- change from a 'mild' to a 'fiercer' competitive market environment.

These are the factors identified by top management and the key informants as to why a culture change was perceived as necessary. The firms under investigation, apart from BAA, were going through a 'crisis', showing a decline in profitability, when the process of culture change was launched. They were struggling for survival (BNFL, BA) or to protect themselves from a takeover (Jaguar). It seems that the company's economic situation dictates the need for a culture change. This can be well illustrated by Schein's (1983b) observation that:

Corporate culture becomes an issue mainly under one condition: the corporation runs into economic difficulties forcing key managers to re-evaluate their culture (p. 25).

Gordon (1985) emphasises similar issues and considers that corporate culture undergoes major change when environmental factors change. He illustrates this point with the case of AT&T, whose culture changed as a consequence of US Government legislation.

> AT&T operated very effectively for 100 years with a single well defined culture. Only when its basic mission was changed by the various arms of the Government did the leaders begin to question the viability of that culture (p. 104).

One of the assumptions at the outset of this research was that privatization (as one aspect of the environment) instigates cultural transformation. However, in effect, such cultural transformation comes from top management's perceptions of environmental change. This can be illustrated by the different ways CEOs reacted to similar external pressures. For example, in BA, the supervisors and first line employees were exposed to training programmes in order to change their own personal values (see figure 11). BAA's top management reacted differently, they emphasised the change in managers' responsibilities. BNFL top management, in turn, emphasised the criteria by which senior management should be selected and promoted.

Jaguar	BNFL	BA	BAA
• New CEO	• New CEO	• New CEO	• New CEO
• New mission	• New mission	• New mission	• New mission
• Basic training (quality circles)	• Major structural modifications	• Basic training (put customer first)	• Major structural modifications
	• New criteria for selecting senior managers	• Minor structural modifications (in few areas)	

Figure 11 Steps of culture change process

Steps in the process of culture change

Although the strategy these four companies utilised to 'change' the culture differed, some steps of this process of change were similar: 1) the appointment of a new CEO, 2) the establishment of a new organizational mission (see figure 11).

I learned through this research that when major changes in the environment are perceived, the transformational leader articulates a new organizational mission. The four case studies revealed that changing mission is an important step in the process of culture change. Hence, as a result of my experience in the field work, I have altered my initial framework to incorporate the concept of organizational mission. That is the reason why mission concept is discussed here for the first time in the book.

The establishment of an organizational mission is one of the most important and most difficult tasks of the organizational leader, according to Tichy (1982) and Tunstall (1983). Denison (1990) considers that mission is a shared definition of the function and purpose of an organization and its members. He also points out that:

> A mission provides purpose and meaning, as well as a host of non economic reasons why the work of an organization is important. It also provides clear direction and goals that serve to define the appropriate course of action for the organization and its members (p. 13).

Tichy (1982), suggests that the establishment of an organizational mission is accomplished by:

1 assessing the environmental threats and opportunities facing the organization.
2 assessing organizational strengths and weaknesses.
3 establishing of the content of the organization's appropriate culture.

The last step is explored in this section, i.e. the way leaders determine what values should be shared; what objectives are worth striving for and what beliefs employees should be committed to.

The role of leaders in determining new missions, and consequently their major task in reshaping corporate culture, has been mentioned by different organizational behaviour theorists. Schein (1985a), for example, dedicated an entire book, *Organizational Culture and Leadership,* to this issue.

> Culture and leadership, when one examines them closely, are two sides of the same coin and neither can really be understood by itself. In fact, there is a possibility - under emphasised in leadership research - that the only thing of real importance that leaders do is to create and manage culture and that the unique talent of leaders is *their ability to work with culture* (p. 5) (my emphasis).

The way in which different CEOs interpret the new external environmental demands seems to be a relevant factor in understanding how a new mission is established, and consequently how culture changes. Therefore, the need for a culture change seems to be determined by the way top management perceive the external environment and the way they decide to react to it. As Schein (1985a) and Fitzgerald (1988) point out, people react not to the objective

91

world but to a world fashioned out of their own perceptions, assumptions and theories of what the world is like.

As shown in fig 11, modifications in the organizational structure seem to be a common step employed by BNFL, BA and BAA. However, BAA top management gave much more emphasis to this aspect than did the other two firms. According to the managers, this strategy was active in terms of culture change. For instance, BAA managers changed their attitudes (becoming more 'complete managers') as a consequence of their new responsibilities which came as a result of a new structure (decentralisation of human resources activities). Similarly in BNFL, senior managers reported that cutting down the layers in the organizational structure facilitated the communication between different levels of managers within the company. One can therefore hypothesise that culture change follows structural change.

Privatization and culture change

As a consequence of the privatization decision, top management in each company tried to reshape their 'historical culture' as a way perceived by them to survive within the new environmental economic constraint. The first step in the process of reshaping their historical culture was the establishment of a new 'core mission'.

Figure 12 shows the historical and prevailing organizational core mission in these four firms. The data was gathered during the interviews, whilst discussing such issues as organizational goals, core values and processes of change. Therefore, the interpretation of the corporate missions is a result of consensus among interviewees and this was validated by official documentation when available.

In the past, Jaguar, BNFL and BA have had similar missions which mainly emphasised the technical aspects of the organization. Lack of commercial awareness, as revealed in the culture, reflects their historical core mission. During the privatization period Jaguar, BNFL and BA share a prevailing mission with emphasis on the market (figure 12).

BNFL's core mission, in the past, was rooted in being a benevolent organization (offering lower grade jobs to the local community) combined with being in the forefront of a high technology industry (hiring 'scientists' from Oxbridge) with the aim of being perfect in terms of technology. BNFL's prevailing mission is to be safe and profitable. Although this change in mission did not appear in official formal documents (as in BA), people in the company (at least at the level I interviewed, senior and middle managers), felt the new mission is emerging gradually, as day to day life is changing, 'the way we do things here is gradually changing'. The mission now, as detailed by various managers, is to be a profitable organization in order to compete both

92

nationally and internationally and, consequently, to be able to survive'. Jaguar has changed its mission from an engineering bias to a market orientated one. BA changed from being an excellent company regarding operations, to become the 'number one' in profits in European airlines.

	Historical	Prevailing
Jaguar	• To produce perfect cars in style and quality (Engineering biased)	• To be a commercial organisation (Market oriented)
BNFL	• To be a safe organisation and provide jobs for community (Paternalist, technical biased)	• To be a safe and profitable organisation (Market orientated)
BA	• To be a reliable airline (Introvert, technical biased)	• To be a customer orientated organisation (Extrovert)
		• To be 'the best' airline
BAA	• To provide good service	• To be profitable
	• To be profitable (Customer orientated)	• To provide good service (Change in emphasis)

Figure 12 The changes in core mission

BAA, however, always had a mission to be profitable and looking at costs was always their concern. Making profits was never considered 'a sin'. BAA moved away from being an organization which emphasised services and profits to becoming a firm which emphasises profits and services. They did not change direction but simply the emphasis.

Managers in BAA challenge the government idea that privatization is a means to make the organization more commercially oriented or more successful.

In my opinion, privatization does not make any company successful. What is necessary is to establish the right culture. That culture is possible in a nationalised industry. However, few nationalised industries could be compared with BAA. There are the founders, the history, we are lucky because we are in a growing industry and also because we had an open minded chairman. We had the opportunity to grow. We reacted to the environment by not being passive. We asked for Gatwick, now we are a monopoly in London.

Ideally, as explained in the literature, when the mission changes, the culture follows it in order to be consistent. However, in practice, it does not always happen like this. Although the four companies established new missions to fit new external demands, the culture itself did not change automatically in the way some CEOs expected. The reason for this 'resistance' seems to be rooted in the history of each company and the CEO's leadership style. Therefore, although all companies held similar prevailing missions (market/business oriented) the prevailing cultures are very different, reflecting different difficulties. To change a culture to be consistent with the core mission seems to be a very complex issue and there follows a description of the way these four companies changed their mission and culture.

   * In Jaguar, a lot of difficulties arose because of their new mission. John Egan, the new CEO, appointed to help the firm in the process of privatization, wanted to implement Total Quality Management (TQM), a corporate strategy which fitted with his new mission (to be market oriented). However, this new corporate strategy, according to top management, requires mainly 'team work' and managerial 'commercial attitudes'. Jaguar's historical culture, however, is characterised by managers as being very 'individualistic' and 'engineering biased'. It seems that the CEO devoted little or no effort to reshaping the culture effectively to fit the new strategy. It became clear, then, that Jaguar could not implement strategies (and ultimately accomplish the new mission) which ran against powerful cultural assumptions. As Schein (1984a) says:

> Not only is it difficult for the ex engineer to conceive of marketing in the way that the professional marketeer perceives this function, but the implementation of a marketing strategy may be undermined by the values and beliefs of people who are in the organization, the incentives systems operating, the issues that executives pay attention to and so on (p. 8).

   * A different type of problem was encountered during the transformation of BA's mission and culture. In the BA case study, the new leader, although aware of the need to change organizational values and beliefs, had a strategy to change culture which emphasised changing people's own values first (via sensitivity training laboratories aimed initially at the lowest levels of the organization). He overlooked the organization's values, i.e. top management's new mindsets. This is typical when the mission has been deliberately changed (through huge campaigns, brochures, and 'lip service'), whilst the culture is resistant to change. This reinforces Wilkins & Patterson's (1985) findings:

> With few exceptions, we see companies going through the exercise of writing a philosophy statement and glossy brochures to announce that the culture is changing, and actually, they keep doing the same things as before... (p. 32).

Another crucial issue that came out of this research is the importance of achieving consensus (by top management) on the 'appropriate' mission and 'appropriate' corporate culture. When consensus is not achieved, a 'split' culture is perceived by managers. For example, in BA two different messages regarding mission and culture are received by managers. The CEO and the Human Resources Director made special efforts to 'force' people to accept the new mission. They arranged seminars, training courses and also pamphlets to deliver the message of the new mission: 'instead of being an excellent aircraft operation company, we are trying to be a "customer service" organization in order to be the best airline in the world, a caring company, which treats passengers well and understands their needs'. Although the intention of BA's CEO is to change the culture to make it consistent with the new mission, it has been a difficult task. As they say, 'people catch the media not the message'. The media, coming from different middle/senior managers, says that they do not want to change the mission nor the culture at all.

Communication, a key issue in the culture change process

Communication is the key issue in the culture change process as revealed by the results of this research. Trying to impose a new way of doing things just through new mission statements proved inefficient as regards culture change strategy. A vital factor in the process of implementing changes seems to be open discussion about the 'needs for a change' with different layers of the organization, starting from the top. It consists of providing information about the new environmental constraints. A participative style of management of change is required. As Jaques (1951) points out, communication includes not only verbal statements and instructions, but non verbal and behavioural messages. The following quotation illustrates this idea:

> Communication is the sum total of directly and indirectly, consciously and unconsciously transmitted feelings, attitudes and wishes which come from the top management (p. 44).

Driver and Coombes (1983), discussing the role of communications in the process of culture change, point out that:

> One of the easiest ways to destroy the confidence that employees have in any change effort, and thereby damn the change to failure, is to allow inconsistent messages about the change to be communicated (p. 35).

This inconsistency in the communications mentioned by Driver and Coombes was evident especially when analysing BA's case study. As explained in detail

95

in Chapter 5, a 'split' situation regarding 'the way managers are expected to behave' was observed in interviews in BA. It might be a reflection of top management's split views regarding the appropriate organizational culture. The majority of board members do not accept the CEO.

In BAA, a similar phenomenon regarding inconsistency in communicating new cultures was perceived by managers. BAA's new mission was to become more profit oriented and the CEO tried to push the organization 'too much' toward profits. As the main values of BAA were profits and services, different messages regarding the appropriate culture were coming from the board. The CEO had serious problems in being accepted by the organization as a whole. Morale went down and key managers were leaving the organization. This CEO left BAA just two years after his appointment.

Whereas in Jaguar, BA and BAA, the process of culture change was more drastic regarding communicating new messages, BNFL seems to be experiencing a smoother transitional phase. It might be a consequence of a 'non imposed new mission'. Top management in BNFL seem to have reached a consensus regarding an appropriate new mission. The strategy of culture change seems to have been developed 'top-down', in a participative way, as described by managers interviewed. Effective communication seems to be the key issue in successfully implementing a culture change programme.

How culture change impinges on managerial careers

The way culture influences careers in Jaguar, BNFL, BA and BAA is illustrated in this section. It is also discussed by Davis and Easterby-Smith (1985). They point out that the values and beliefs shared by top management groups exert a significant influence on the way managers are recruited, selected, promoted and rewarded. They argue that:

> The process of recruitment, selection and promotion ensures that only people who fit in with the dominant culture are allowed to enter and remain in an organization... Thus, the whole HR system is still geared to select only those who fit in with the existing view of what is effective management and of who is likely to be an effective manager. The selectors tend to identify characteristics in individuals which support the main myths (p. 23).

The findings of this research not only confirm Davis and Easterby-Smith's theoretical views, but they add a 'processual' perspective to their ideas. In companies experiencing the process of culture change, the whole human resources system will be geared to select, promote, reward only those who fit in with the desired/appropriate culture. Therefore it seems that managerial skills and attitudes vary according to the organizational change process.

Based on the experience gained in this research, two figures were created in order to clarify the process of culture change and its relationships with

96

managerial careers. Figure 13 displays the impact of culture change on careers - before privatization (historically). Figure 14 displays the impact of culture change on careers - during privatization.

Figure 13 shows that the organizational culture influences the way managers are expected to behave and consequently the managerial career systems.

Figure 14 shows that, when changes in the environment are perceived by top management, a new mission is established and, as a result, new culture and new management behaviour are required. New career systems are then designed (the new criteria companies use to select, promote, redirect training and development and reward) reflecting a new culture.

The next two sections analyse the impact of historical and of prevailing culture on managerial careers, based on the empirical data obtained in these four companies.

The impact of historical culture on managers' careers - pre privatization

The way managers were expected to behave in the past differed in these four companies as a reflection of each individual organization's historical culture. As a consequence of those cultural differences, successful and deviant managers differed in the past from one organization to another. For example, a 'thoughtful' and 'relaxed' manager would be considered a deviant in Jaguar's historical culture and a 'dynamic' or 'aggressive' manager would be considered a deviant in BNFL. By and large, a generalist manager would not 'get on' in BNFL's historical culture, whereas a specialist manager would not 'get on' in BAA's historical culture. Evidence for these statements is given in each individual case study.

Figure 15 displays the summary of findings related to the links between culture and careers, historically in Jaguar, BNFL, BA and BAA. Both careers and culture seem to be unique for each organization. A few generalisations, however, are made below:

* Jaguar, BNFL and BA tended to be technically biased, that is, towards engineering. Consequently, the criteria utilised by these three companies to select/promote/reward managers reflected this cultural feature. Additionally, training was geared mainly to technical specialisation.

* In BNFL, managers in the past were required to be innovative in technical terms, rather than in administrative terms. Perfectionism in technical terms was always the aim whereas 'an eye on costs' was never an issue in BNFL's historical culture.

* BAA managers have always considered themselves as commercially oriented. The training for generalists and selection criteria based on creativity innovation and communication skills reinforce this.

* In BA, the historical culture was characterised as political and technically biased and this was reinforced by selection according to technical skills and promotion based on seniority and 'who knows whom'.

* BNFL, BA and BAA, as a reflection of a civil service bureaucracy, used to reward managers on seniority (length of service).

* The common trait of historical managerial career systems in BNFL and BA, (also BAA during the first ten years of its existence, i.e. before the new MD was appointed), is observed in the recruitment process. Jobs historically were advertised as reflecting the 'hard but fair' type of civil service values and beliefs. Managers, with little information about the requirements of the job, applied and were often disappointed and frustrated to be exposed to panel interviews where they became aware that the person for the job had already been chosen. However, in keeping with the bureaucratic type of culture, these procedures took time to be replaced. This type of practice has been gradually abolished, as it was regarded as 'inefficient'. Now, appropriate potential candidates tend to be appointed by the human resources department. This change was noticed more clearly in BNFL and BAA case studies.

In summary, although some of the criteria these companies used to select, promote and reward were similar (e.g. technical competence), the 'cultural package' as a whole was unique for each case. That means, every company was unique in its historical culture and, consequently, in its historical career systems.

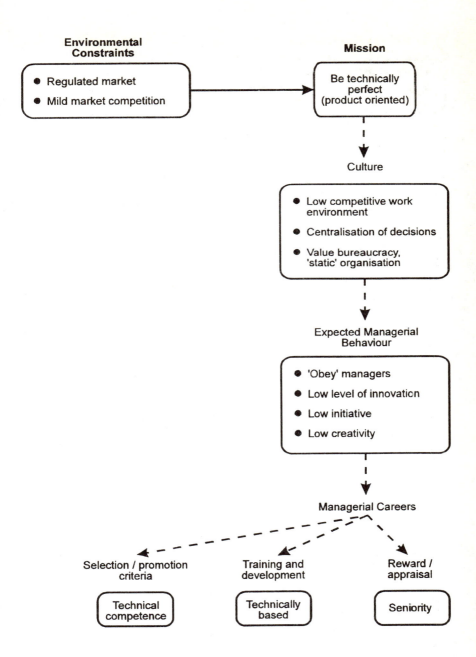

Figure 13   The impact of culture on managerial careers (before privatization)

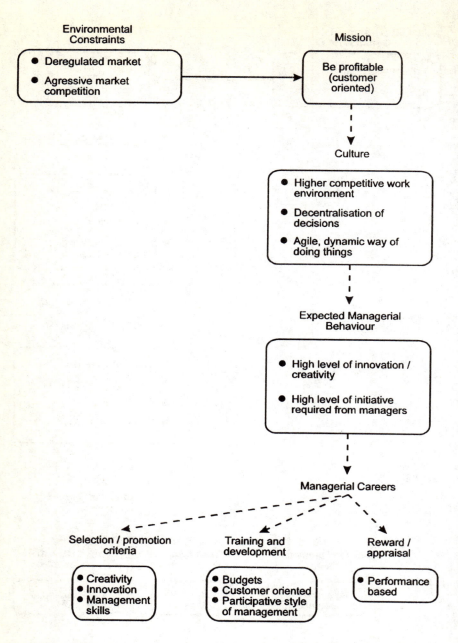

Figure 14   The impact of culture on managerial careers (after privatization)

Features of culture

Career systems

	Features of culture	Criteria for selection	Training/development	Reward
Jaguar • Authoritarian • Dynamic	• Drive • Dynamism • Authoritarian • Engineering biased	• 'Hard worker' • Technical competency • Drive, dynamism • Authoritarian • Work in isolation	• Specialisation	• Based on criteria for selection/promotion
BNFL • 'Inward looking'	• Secrecy • Bureaucracy • Perfectionism • Paternalism • Engineering biased	• 'Relaxing worker' • Thoughtful person • High IQ • High educational level (Oxford and Cambridge) • Low initiative – obey manager • Technical competency	• Specialisation	• Technical competence • Seniority
BA • 'Inward looking'	• Engineering biased • Security • Political • Formality • Bureaucracy	• Who knows who • Technical competency • Seniority	• Specialisation	• Technical competence • Seniority
BAA • 'Outward looking'	• Commerically biased • Flexibility • Innovation • Openness	• Initiative • Innovative • Flexibility • Communication skills	• Generalist • Team work • Participative style • Initiativity • Communication skills	• Communication skills • Seniority

Figure 15 Culture and careers - historical analysis

All four organizations have, to some extent changed their career systems as a consequence of the emergence of a new corporate culture. The transition from a government owned organization to a private company was noticeable in these four companies, especially in BNFL, BA and BAA. This can be observed by the way managers perceive the prevailing culture and prevailing managerial careers. The environment in which these four firms now operate is very different from what it was in the past: without financial support from the Government, they all have to struggle to keep their position in the market place.

Today the links between prevailing culture and careers are not as clear as they were historically. That is because the companies under investigation are still experiencing a transitional phase. Therefore, although in certain circumstances those links were quite clear (as in BAA), in others, I found split values, (as in BA) in both prevailing culture and career systems.

Figure 16 displays the summary of findings related to the impact of culture on careers in Jaguar, BNFL, BA and BAA. The common aspect of all four companies is that they are trying to become more competitive. Career moves for managers, in all four companies investigated, are much faster than before, i.e. younger managers are promoted to higher positions regardless of the number of years of working for the company. The idea of promotion according to seniority is being gradually abolished.

Although common traits were found in prevailing culture and careers when comparing and contrasting these four companies, the process of change in itself was very different. Those differences are shown below:

* In Jaguar, although the mission has changed, the culture and career systems remain roughly unchanged. A comparative analysis between figure 15 and figure 16, illustrates this statement. It can be observed that although the environment has changed and a new CEO been appointed, Jaguar's culture seems to remain constant. Managers interviewed described the 'appropriate managerial behaviour' as team work, thoughtfulness and more planning than action. However, the criteria for selecting newcomers remained entrenched in the old values (technician, working in isolation, dynamism). Training and development, however, has been modified: they are sending managers to MBA courses and also rotate junior managers in different departments in order to broaden their views of the business. Quality circles have been implemented, although unsuccessfully, as seen by managers. As one manager commented:

Features of culture

Career systems

	Features of culture	Selection/Promotion	Training/Development	Rewards
Jaguar • Authoritarian • Dynamic	• Drive • Dynamism • Authoritarian • Engineering biased • Individualism *Old values*	• 'Hard worker' • Technical competency • Drive, dynamism • Authoritarian, style • Work in isolation *Old values*	• MBM • Rotate managers	Based on criteria for selection/ promotion *Old values*
BNFL • 'Outward looking'	• Participation • Initiative • Openness • Innovation *New values*	• Initiative • Creativity • Not obey managers • Excellent leaders *New values*	• Rotate managers • MBA *New values*	Performance based (targets) *New values*
BA • 'Split values'	• Authoritarian x participation • Team work x isolated jobs • Technical biased x commercial biased • Informality x formality *Split values*	• Technical competence x people management skills *Split procedures*	• Put customers first • Be participative • Team work *New values*	Technical biased criteria x 'people management skills' *Split procedures*
BAA • 'Outward looking'	• Financially biased • Flexibility • Innovation • Openness *Gradual evolution*	• Financial skills • Innovative • Flexibility • Initiativity	• Generalist • Team work • Participative style • Initiativity • Budgeting	Based on performance (emphasis on financial skills)

Figure 16 Culture and careers - prevailing analysis

Within an authoritarian culture, it is almost impossible to develop quality circles where team work and a participatory style is a must.

* In BNFL, the mission, culture and careers are changing radically to fit the new external environment. Their process of culture change (from historical to prevailing) emphasises the selection and promotion of senior executives. It can be illustrated by the following quote from a BNFL interviewee:

I used to be considered a deviant in the historical culture as I was always willing to introduce changes in the routine of my work. Nevertheless, because of this same trait, I have just recently been appointed a senior manager.

* In BA, some departments seem to operate under new values, however, others are operating under old values: there is a 'split' situation. There is an inconsistent corporate culture.

* In BAA, the mission, culture and careers are slightly changed to emphasise financial skills in a consistent way. The prevailing culture is becoming more finance oriented than in the past. Consequently, financial skills have been incorporated into BAA's career systems.

Human resources philosophy in BA/Jaguar and BAA/BNFL: a contrast

Human resources philosophy differentiates BAA/BNFL from BA/Jaguar in the transition from the historical to the prevailing period. On one hand, in BA and Jaguar it tends to reinforce the idea that it is necessary to change people's values to fit the new mission/culture. BAA and BNFL, on the other hand, believe that 'role modelling' and changing people's responsibilities as a consequence of organizational structural change will provoke the required management behaviour modifications.

Almost everyone can change as long as we give them a different framework and a different work situation, and provide them with the necessary tools to do a different job.

Managerial careers: tools to change corporate culture

The literature in human resources management tends to emphasise the importance of career systems as tools which managers can use to change culture. For example, Kerr (1987) points out that a careful consideration of career systems represents the basis for the process of culture change. Schneider (1988), in her theoretical article, states that:

Corporate culture is managed through human resources management practices (p. 232).

The results of this research, however, challenge both Kerr's (1987) and Schneider's (1988) findings. It appears that human resources efforts (selection, training, promotion, and rewards), in isolation, are not powerful enough to provoke a 'culture change' (Easterby-Smith, 1988). The culture change process appears to lie with the company's leadership. As said by Gordon (1985), every organization is the lengthened shadow of its leaders. He considers that if a company wishes to modify its culture, the thrust must come from the top:

> It is they (the leaders) who set the direction, reinforce the values, and raise the consciousness of the organization to what it must be rather than what it has been (p. 87).

It became clear during the field work process that human resources management is crucial in the process of culture change. However, by human resources management the interviewees meant the activities regarding employees administered by line managers. The role of personnel in influencing selection, training and rewards was considered to be irrelevant since the personnel department usually lacks information about 'real' organizational needs or about the specific sub cultures of each department.

The 'powerlessness' of personnel functions has already been mentioned by Angle et al. (1985). They argue that there is a 'tradition', mainly in large organizations, for line management to over delegate the care of the organization's human resources to the personnel staff. This tendency was highlighted also in Townsend's (1971), in which he advised that many organizations would be better off abolishing the personnel functions altogether. Firing the personnel manager, he implied, would force line managers to face up to their 'people problems' rather than 'shunting them off to personnel'.

The tendency to decentralise the personnel functions has been observed clearly in this research, especially in BA and BAA. For example, in BAA, a very clear and well described transition from centralisation to decentralisation has been reported by managers regarding personnel structures during the process of culture change. Personnel, in the past, used to be the most powerful department in BAA. Now, as a result of gradual culture changes, following the implementation of the new mission in which the firm is trying to be more profit oriented, the finance area has become the most powerful function. Personnel functions have been delegated to the different subsidiaries. Consequently, a required change in managerial behaviour has been accomplished, as reported by managers. They can be considered now as 'more complete managers'.

In BA, however, this issue has only recently been tackled. Their first attempt to change culture (and ultimately to change managerial behaviour) was through the personnel function. The CEO hired 'a very strong and dominating HR director' in order to implement culture changes. But this strategy of centralising the personnel activities did not work as expected: after a period of two years, the Human Resources Director was forced to leave the organization and a process of decentralisation was then initiated in BA. According to an internal auditor:

> In my opinion, we only need one person in HR area, an adviser, all this heavy and populous human resource structure should go.

To summarise, whereas career management has been considered by the literature as 'tools to change corporate culture', the findings of this research do not confirm this statement. The study suggests that managerial careers, in isolation, are not powerful enough to change culture.

Summary

This chapter has focused on exploring the similarities and the differences regarding the culture change process associated with the privatization decision in Jaguar, BNFL, BA and BAA.

The cross case analysis highlights four important steps for a 'successful' culture change process:

1 The appointment of a CEO.
2 The establishment of a new core mission.
3 Modifications in the organizational structure.
4 Reshaping of managerial careers.

None of these steps in isolation, however, can bring the expected result. An integration of these actions seems to be the key for a strategic culture change. The employee involvement at all levels of the organizational structure, starting from the top, was revealed to be a crucial element in the way the CEO implemented the necessary actions. Participative rather than authoritarian style proved more efficient for the achievement of consistency in culture change process.

As shown in this chapter, the links between culture and careers are organizational specific, i.e. the way careers are managed in each organization reflects its own particular culture. Some generalisations, however, can be drawn when comparing and contrasting the way managerial careers changed in these companies during the privatization period.

Career progress, historically in all four companies, tended to be slow if compared to the present. Furthermore, in the past, managers were appraised and rewarded according to seniority. After the privatization decision, however, appraisal and reward systems became performance related.

Jaguar, BNFL and BA managers, in the past, were selected and promoted according to their technical skills. After the privatization decision, however, there is an attempt to select and promote managers according to their commercial skills. By contrast with Jaguar, BA and BNFL, commercial awareness has always been a managerial requirement within BAA corporate culture.

BAA's culture change process differs significantly from the three previous case studies: this company has always been in the process of gradual change as a way to follow the constant environmental changes. As a reflection of this, managerial careers have gradually been undergoing modifications.

7 Usiminas: The Brazilian case study

Introduction

The privatization procedure in Brazil began in 1990, with the inclusion of Usiminas in the Brazilian Denationalisation Program by means of Decree Number 99494 of August 1990. Usiminas is the domestic market leader in the steel sector and supplies forty two per cent of domestic demand. It operates under an integrated system, which includes the processing of the iron ore and coal to the transformation into rolled steel.

The Brazilian privatization programme is an essential part of the structural reforms introduced in 1990 by President Collor's Government. These reforms, via economic stability and the recuperation of public finances through fiscal adjustment, aim at modernising the Brazilian economy and paving the way for economic growth recovery and a higher standard of living for the Brazilian population. The Brazilian privatization programme allows the Government to focus resources and efforts into areas such as education, health, housing, security and sanitation where its presence is essential, contributing to redefine the role of the state in the Brazilian economy.

This case explores the transitional phase Usiminas experienced when it became private in 1991. The overall contribution of this study lies in revealing how Usiminas went through the process of replacing their historical values, in order to survive within the new economic environment, which resulted from the privatization decision in Brazil. Specifically it analyses the 'old' and 'new' organizational values and how these new values impinged on human resource management and on organizational structure.

A briefing on Usiminas: a Brazilian steel organization

Usiminas was created in 1956 in the State of Minas Gerais in Brazil.

Since its foundation, Usiminas has always operated under the control of the state. Usiminas has facilities, including warehouses, at locations across Brazil (eleven) and in Japan (one). As at 30 April 1992, Usiminas employed a total of 13,547 people in the headquarters, plants, regional offices and warehouses. The purpose of the firm is to exploit the steel and related industries, sell, import and export steel products and byproducts and raw materials, carry out and design projects and research, train technicians, and exploit mining, transport, construction and technical assistance activities. The company was the first joint venture of Japanese industry in the western world after World War II. Its success went a long was to proving Japanese competence just when Japan was beginning to export technology.

Usiminas is the leading company on the Brazilian market and it is competitive internationally. The competitiveness of Usiminas on the domestic market is demonstrated by its greater technical operational productivity, lower levels of structural expenses and of financial indebtedness than other Brazilian plants.

Usiminas sells more than seventy per cent of its production directly to consumers on the domestic market. Its most regular international markets are the United States, Japan, China, South Korea, Singapore and Malaysia. Its products are well accepted on the international market.

Usiminas was chosen by President Collor's Government to launch the privatization programme in Brazil.

Method

Adopting Andrew Pettigrew's (1979) perspective in this research, it was assumed that an organization may profitably be explored as a continuous system, with a past, a present and a future. Organizations shift in response to market environment or social forces. These shifts are hard to detect when they occur, but they are easy to recognise in retrospect through each organization's passages and history. Learning to identify these events was part of my task as a researcher. The process itself, as explained by Pettigrew (1979), is seen as a continuous interdependent sequence of actions and events that can be used to explain the origins, continuations, and outcome of some phenomenon. The focus is as much on the process of becoming as on that of being. See figure 17 for the framework utilised in this study.

110

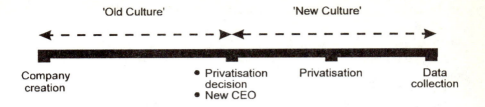

Figure 17 Theoretical framework (a)

Data collection and analysis

Twenty two semi structured interviews with middle and senior management across departments were conducted during 1992. These interviews aimed to understand how managers perceived the process of change in Usiminas. Each meeting lasted approximately one hour. They took place at the headquarters and at the plant. I addressed questions regarding the process of change. This involved enquiries about leaders' values, the historical and prevailing expected managerial behaviour, core mission, human resource practices (career management in particular) and organizational structure. One question which instigated interesting answers was the one about Usiminas 'personality' in this change process. An interpretative paradigm was utilized to analyse the data collected.

Historical period: the Usiminas 'old values'

A retrospective approach was considered appropriate as I was interested in the present managers' perceptions of the past. The aim was to investigate how managers, as a group, perceived the historical events and how this contributes to their better understanding of their own organizations.

   Usiminas has always been a successful organization.

   A company that succeeded.

As seen by managers interviewed, most of the success of Usiminas is due to the fact that their founder and first leader remained in the post as CEO for almost two decades. Therefore, in their eyes, there was a continuity in management terms which did not occur in other Brazilian government organizations.

   In the past, the core mission of Usiminas was:

111

1   'To produce' in order to respond to the high demand from the internal market.

2.   'To socialise' the town of Ipatinga where the plant lies.

Usiminas' culture is a product of the synergy between Japanese and Brazilian values.   As the main management training took place in Japan, Usiminas employees learned to be 'disciplined'.   There was a high respect for the hierarchy - 'nobody could question the superior'.   The company was described as authoritarian.   The interviewees considered that this trait reflected the Brazilian former dictatorship system.

I found consensus regarding Usiminas' organizational culture before privatization.   This has been described as:

Insulated, oppressed, paternalistic, bureaucratic, authoritarian.

The paternalism was a barrier to developing a new organizational structure.

We never changed the structure because we did not want to hurt people...   we always wanted to protect the employees.

People used to spend a great amount of time in preparing reports, 'usefulness figures' and 'absurd' controls which were requested by the Government.   These bureaucratic activities, according to the managers, were a block in both the organizational systems and structure.

Very bureaucratic...   Everything and everybody were under rigid control... reports, papers...

The decision process was slow as the power was centralised.   In the past, employees would work in teams within areas but not across areas.   Each department used to work in isolation from the others.

Prevailing period: the Usiminas 'new values'

Usiminas, in 1992, was in the midst of a programme for technological modernization aimed at upgrading its product line, improving quality, and using to the fullest the productive capacity of its installations, in order to be, as a result, competitive on the domestic and foreign markets.

Usiminas top management realised that a 'culture change' was necessary for the organizational survival and growth as an independent enterprise. Although they felt that some corporate values were changing (such as bureaucracy), few of the 'old' ones must be kept (loyalty).   They stated that the company was becoming more 'customer' orientated (instead of 'product' orientated) and to minimise costs was a must.

The commercial area has been perceived as the one which was undergoing major changes: it is more flexible, dynamic, agile. The sales department is freer to establish the product prices. The purchasing department now works under less costs as many bureaucratic procedures have been eliminated after privatization.

The company is trying to move from authoritarian to participative management style. 'The manager works to help the team and not vice versa' as shown below.

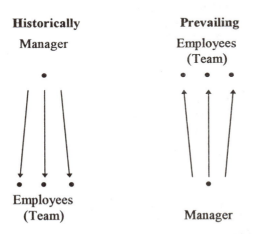

The company is trying to involve employees in all activities. For instance, whereas in the past the manager would travel abroad to solve some specific issues with the customers, today people from operations do the overseas travelling. Historically, management power would come from his/her position. Prevailing, it comes from his/her own leadership style.

Managers have mentioned the importance of self actualization through work. With more involvement, more responsibility for results, more freedom to make decisions, managers would feel happier in their own jobs.

Usiminas was communicating to the employees the need for achieving company results. In the past, the emphasis was placed on each department's results.

Management in Usiminas is becoming aware of the organization's possibilities (its strengths) and limitations (its weaknesses).

The outlook for the company is now considered optimistic. It is seeking to place itself among the most successful companies in the world.

The impact of privatization on human resource management and on organization structure

a) Human resource management

Human resource practices both reflect and reinforce the corporate culture (Schein, 1988; Payne, 1991; Salama, 1991). This is very clear in the Usiminas case study, i.e. the historical and prevailing values of the company were reflected in and reinforced by the historical and prevailing human resource practices. This phenomenon is shown in the figures 18 and 19 and is explained in detail in the following paragraphs.

When the organization belonged to the Government, there was no freedom to employ and dismiss people or to establish a salary policy. The managers were expected to follow the Government's rules and procedures regarding personnel. For instance it was up to the President of the Republic to give the final approval for someone to undertake a course abroad. All these old procedures have been modified. The salary now is not linked to Government approval anymore. Therefore, the system became more flexible and consequently fairer, according to the managers' accounts.

Culture	Human resource management			
	Selection	Training	Rewards/ Promotion	Salary
Strong	Only people with no experience	Specialisation	Specialists	
Homogenous	No 'buy out'			
Paternalism			Job for life	
Authoritarian			'Obey managers'	
Traditional			Seniority	
Production orientation	Technical skills	Technical orientation		
Bureaucratic controlled				Tied to government

Figure 18 Historical analysis - Usiminas

114

Culture	Human resource management			
	Selection	Training	Rewards/ Promotion	Salary
Diversity	People with outside experience	Rotate managers	Generalists	
Towards results			Performance related	
Participative	Leadership skills	Management training		
Innovative	Creativity		Creativity	
Profit orientated		Finance courses	Performance related	
Commercial biased			Customer orientated	
Team orientated			Achieving company's results	
Freedom				Performance related

Figure 19 Prevailing analysis - Usiminas

Recruitment/selection The recruitment used to be from schools/universities. The criteria for bringing in new employees was technical skills and academic curriculum. No previous experience was required as the employees would undertake a series of training within the organization. This type of policy would reinforce the strengths of Usiminas *culture*. Today the company is trying to diversify the type of people they hire in order to get a more heterogeneous work force. The selection criteria has been changed. Today managers are looking for people with experience in other companies, a different profile.

We are changing the man with boots into those with ties.

Training Usiminas historically used internal resources to train its employees because of the particularities of steel making, and works to maintain a high standard of training among its employees. The company participates in a variety of international programmes for technology transfer that include foreign travel by technicians. More than five million hours have been spent in personnel training, involving more than 200,000 participants in courses of various levels, both in Brazil and abroad.

Although the training department has not suffered significant changes as a consequence of the privatization decision, top managers are aware of the need to enhance management training and development.

> We need to create leaders not only technicians.

However, *how* to change management behaviour/attitudes is still a 'grey' area for Usiminas. They are aware of the need to move managers towards becoming generalists. Financial aspects now are vital for the decision making process.

Career management Reflecting the historical culture, careers were developed at a slow rate and within functional areas. People would stay in the same job for many years as the employee turnover was extremely low. For instance, one manager I interviewed remained in the same function (R&D) for twenty two years. Now, they cannot stay more than five years in one job. Career management, although not responsible for provoking culture changes alone, is revealed as playing an important role in reinforcing new managerial attitudes and consequently gradually reshaping the corporate culture. By and large, managers are now being selected, promoted, trained and rewarded differently compared with before the privatization. These modifications in career management reflected the changes in the way managers were expected to behave when major organizational changes occurred.

b) Usiminas' organizational structure

Managers agreed that Usiminas systems and procedures ought to become more flexible and agile. They also considered that the structure needed to have a flatter shape. A major organizational structure change was in the process of implementation in order to facilitate this behaviour change.

Summary

Matching the UK case studies' results (see Chapter 5), the process of culture change in Usiminas has been managed with the use of three tools: new core mission, organizational structure change and new human resource practices.

The mission was moving from production to customer orientation. The new structure was trying to simplify procedures and moving down the power decisions. Human resource management was trying to develop the management skills along with technical skills.

It is important to note that the success of the privatization process in Usiminas, according to the managers interviewed, is due to the great emphasis given to the preparation phase, i.e. several meetings involving all levels of staff were conducted explaining with detail each step of the process. Communication and involvement seems to represent facilitator factors in a major process of change (Salama, 1992).

Reinforcing Shein's (1984a) recommendations, the process of culture change in Usiminas respected some of the organization's original values while it is trying to replace others. This can be illustrated by the following quotations:

Usiminas' personality

Before privatization: ...A middle aged serious married woman, traditional, hard worker, intelligent and honourable...

After privatization: ...A nice middle aged single woman, open, who enjoys challenges, dynamic, intelligent, honourable...

It is clear through these quotations that, the privatization helped the company to release its potential which was blocked by the Government's style: centralization of power.

It was found that managers are starting to learn and embrace new ways of doing things. For instance, bureaucracy is gradually being replaced by an appreciation of innovation in management terms. Such transformation, though, can be difficult to accomplish. As the case study demonstrates, corporate culture is deep rooted and complex. The change process itself generates many conflicts, as does the clash between new and old outlooks and behaviour.

It became clear through the accounts that the process of change is slow and that the Usiminas managers are still starting it. Nevertheless, it was clearly a consensus among interviewees that the company as a whole is functioning with more freedom.

Managers feel more responsible for decisions. They are asked to be more dynamic, the decision making process became faster. Managers interviewed considered that the process they are experiencing is more likely to be called an 'evolution' than a 'revolution'.

There were no traumas in this process of culture change.

The process did not try to destroy the 'old culture'.

We worked with the culture not against it...

117

8 Summary and conclusions

This chapter provides an account of the principal findings of the study and places the results within the context of the existing literature. It discusses two main topics: *a) the process of creating corporate culture from the point of view of an empirical investigation; and b) the universal approach to culture change*.

Overview of the findings

The scale of organizational change prompted by privatization provides an ideal focus for the investigation of culture change. However, the lessons learned here are applicable to many organizations facing culture change of this scale and magnitude.

The rationale of the privatization programme is explained as stimulating the economy within the framework of new regulatory mechanisms (Fraser, 1988). As became evident in this book, this programme has increasingly come to be represented in cultural terms, concerned with the attitudes, values and forms of self understanding embedded in both individual and institutional activities.

The overall contribution of this book lies in revealing how Jaguar, BNFL, BA, BAA and Usiminas went through the process of replacing their historical values, in order to survive within the new economic environment which resulted from the privatization decisions. A comparative analysis between these firms was made as well as an integrative model of culture change provided.

The results of this comparison revealed that the new environmental demands followed by privatization (i.e. the fiercer market competition and deregulation) represented major factors which instigated culture change. New CEOs were appointed to prepare the organizations for this 'new era'; new core missions (profitable orientated) and modifications in the organization structure (decentralization) were the two main initial tasks accomplished by the CEOs in each organization. Furthermore, the need for change was communicated to the employees at all levels of the organization. During the process of culture change all companies under investigation modified their personnel practices regarding managerial careers.

It is important to note that the public debate about the privatization programme's merits was not the focus of this book. Rather, it focused on how people within organizations actually perceived the culture changes which had occurred when they were experiencing the transition from state owned to private organizations. It was found that managers are starting to learn and embrace new ways of doing things. For instance, bureaucracy is gradually being replaced by an appreciation of innovation in management terms. Such transformation, though, can be difficult to accomplish. As the case studies demonstrate, corporate cultures are deep rooted and complex. The change process itself generates many conflicts, as does the clash between new and old outlooks and behaviour. Such difficulties in the process of culture change could be minimised, depending upon the strategy adopted by CEO in their programmes of culture change.

Specific findings

This book attempts to enrich the literature on organizational studies in two specific areas:

1   The process of creating corporate culture: an empirical investigation.
2   The process of transforming corporate culture: a universal approach.

1 The process of creating corporate culture

This book analysed empirically the process by which culture originated in these five companies. This was considered to be a fundamental step in understanding fully the process of culture change which represents a central issue of this book. The research demonstrated how five government owned organizations had come to have very different ways of operating. Two elements seemed to play a crucial role in this differentiation:

*   The founders' and past leaders' values.
*   The industry's dominant values (type of technology and its relationship with the environment).

One of the most mysterious aspects of organizational culture is how it originates (Schein, 1985b). Watson (1963) considers that IBM's culture is a pure reflection of its founder:

> The beliefs that mould great organizations frequently grow out of the character, the experiences, and the convictions of a single person... IBM is the reflection of one individual - my father, T.J. Watson (p. 45).

Although the impact of founders' and past leaders' values seems to represent a commonplace in the literature on corporate culture, the importance of an industry's dominant values in forming culture is almost a neglected topic. Very few studies are devoted to the relationship between any specific type of industry (dominant technology) and corporate culture. The findings of this research highlight not only the importance of leaders' values in creating a corporate culture, but also the impact of each specific industry's dominant values on culture. As explained earlier in more detail, the culture in BNFL seems to be influenced by the perfectionism and secrecy of the nuclear industry; in Jaguar by the drive and sophistication of luxury car manufacture; in British Airways by the technical bias of the airline industry; in BAA by commercial awareness of the airport management business; and in Usiminas by the engineer's bias.

2 The process of transforming corporate culture: a universal approach

Using a grounded theory approach (Glaser and Strauss, 1967), this book contributes to the literature on the culture change process. The interesting issues which emerged were related to:

a)   The need for a culture change.
b)   Who leads the culture change process?
c)   The importance of organizational self awareness in the process of culture change.

a) The need for a culture change   Morgan (1988) suggests that the need for change stems from the instability of the external environment. As the socioeconomic world grows more turbulent, an ability to understand one's organization and position it to deal with emerging trends becomes more and more important.

> Few, if any, organizations can now feel secure in their niches (p. 23).

Reinforcing his contextual approach, Handy (1976) argues that the nature of the environment within which an organization works is often taken for granted by those who work within it but it can be crucially important in determining the culture.

The results of this investigation support the ideas of Handy (1976) and Morgan (1988). Additionally, these findings complement their views, since the research incorporates a phenomenological perspective, in which the social world is not viewed as an objective entity, but rather as subjective, based on the individual's perceptions of social events (Schultz, 1970). Therefore, from a phenomenological perspective, one can conclude that the need for a 'major' culture change in these five firms stemmed from top management's perceptions of the privatization process, i.e. their perceptions about the implications of this political action on their market place and consequently, on their economic situation.

Culture, however, is found to be difficult to modify. The reasons for such resistance to culture change lie probably in the strong way that corporate culture was created (see Chapter 4). The culture of an organization tends to remain the same until a change in the environment occurs and threatens its survival. This pervasiveness of culture within organizations was noticeable mainly in Jaguar, BNFL, BA and Usiminas. The results of these four case studies revealed that their culture was 'static' until the decision of privatization was announced. Nevertheless, BAA's case study challenges this idea. In BAA it was found that an innovative type of culture can exist within a nationalized organization. Some managers in BAA deny that privatization, on its own, was helping the organization to be more efficient. They considered that prior to privatization they were already 'quite an efficient organization' and that privatization could not be successful without the foundation of their business - 'a good solid and well run organization culture'. This 'right corporate culture' seems to reflect the top leader's attitude in BAA (see Chapter 5), who has been relatively receptive to constant environmental change.

b) Who leads the culture change process? It was found that, when changes in the environment occur, the top leader articulates new values and norms and then uses multiple change levers ranging from role modelling, and the creation of new rituals, to revamping of human resources systems and management process to support new culture messages.

In these five organizations, new chairmen and/or CEO were appointed to prepare the organizations for privatization. One of the tasks they were expected to pursue was to lead the organization's culture change process. The new CEO/Chairmen then established new organizational missions and reshaped the organizational structure. Additionally they attempted to select/promote top management who held values which matched the 'desired culture'. This is reinforced by Dumain (1990).

Many times history cannot be changed without changing the players (p. 25).

122

The key to culture change appears to lie with the company's leadership (Gordon, 1985; Schein, 1985a). It seems clear that this statement does not apply solely to founders (like Sir John Williams at Jaguar and Sir Norman Payne at BAA). It applies also to the leaders who find it necessary to remodel their companies at any particular point in their history - leaders who have the determination and perseverance to effect change (such as Colin Marshall at BA, Christopher Harding at BNFL and Rinaldo Campos Soares at Usiminas).

Dumain (1990) argues that a CEO must promulgate a vision of desired change and support it with action. He considers that CEOs and top managers should live the culture they want. He means that it is not enough to pay 'lip service' to the required changes, but, most importantly, to behave in the way managers are expected to. As he argued:

As always, actions speak louder than words (p. 58).

To summarise this sub section, it can be concluded that the basic lesson on culture change is that culture change must come from the bottom, but the chief executive officer (CEO) must guide it.

c) The importance of organizational self awareness in the process of culture change According to Schein (1985b), the change theory lies in the following quotation:

Once we become aware we can choose (p. 42).

Drawing issues from these five case studies, it is possible to conclude that awareness of each firm's own culture was the starting point for any modification in organizational culture. The clear descriptions of the historical culture in each case study show that the companies were embarking on the process of knowing themselves. The difficulty, however, in the process of culture change, seems to lie in the question of how to move from the 'historical' culture to the 'appropriate' culture.

Although all companies revealed a good level of awareness of their own historical culture, top management did not always consider it when designing new strategies for their companies. This represented a barrier to the process of culture change. If an organization is to understand its own strengths and weaknesses, and if it is to make informed strategic choices based on realistic assessments of external and internal factors, it must study and understand its own culture. But this process is not without its problems, risks and potential costs. For example, the organization could be made more vulnerable through having its culture revealed to outsiders, (Schein 1985a, p. 139). This fear of exposure was demonstrated by Jaguar when permission was sought to present the research at a US conference (their principal market).

The results of this study reveal that awareness of each organization's historical and existing culture is the starting point for any successfully planned organizational change. This is illustrated by the following quotation:

A company trying to improve its culture is like a person trying to improve his or her character. For this you need to investigate the past (Dumain, 1990, p. 56).

Jaques (1951) raised this issue four decades ago. He considered that studies on culture are relevant for the full understanding of organizational behaviour. He states that, in order to understand the present situation, it is necessary to consider the dynamics of certain outstanding historical events in the life of the organization, events whose definite mark is left on the pattern of the present.

To better understand the importance of the past (historical culture), we can also recall Freud (1940). He considered that past experiences provide insights to patients which help them to carry on their future lives and make better choices. One can argue that companies, like people, are always tied to the past, (Wilkins and Patterson, 1985). Therefore, the 'right manager' may be the one who can understand and respect the organization's historical culture, cope with the prevailing culture, and help the organization to achieve its 'appropriate culture' in the future.

How transferable is the British experience on culture change process?

How much of the experience from the UK can be applied globally? How many of the concepts learned can help managers working in other countries? These were the main questions behind my investigation on Usiminas, a Brazilian steel organization which launched the privatization programme in Brazil. I utilised the integrative model of culture change (figure 1) which had been previously developed based on British data as a framework to understand Usiminas' process of culture change. The model fits with the Brazilian data and this is a positive indication that the concepts could be useful for managers globally provided they consider not only the process but also the influence of national cultural dimensions.

The comparative analysis suggests that there might be a universal way to deal with culture changes within organizations in terms of processes. Regarding the context within which such transitions occur, it might be said that there are great differences between Brazil and Britain. It was found that national cultural dimensions impinged on the implementation of the six steps (figure 1) of strategic culture change.

From the perspective of organizational change, it is important to understand the culture in which one is working. Different countries' value systems impinge on employee's behaviour at the work place. As Hofstede (1980) explains, people carry 'mental programmes' which are developed in the family in early childhood and reinforced in schools and organizations. These mental programmes are most clearly expressed in the different values that predominate among people from different countries.

Differences in national culture can either facilitate or hinder the process of change within organizations. This phenomenon can be illustrated by describing a few examples extracted from this research. Two cultural dimensions played a significant role during the culture change process in the five firms under investigation. These dimensions are Power Distance (PD) and Individualism (IV). I will first explain the concept of each of these two dimensions as described by Hofstede.(1980). Furthermore, I will exemplify how these dimensions impinged on the cultural transitions experienced by Usiminas, Jaguar, BA, BNFL and BAA.

Power distance

This concept was utilised by Hofstede (1980) to describe the relationships between boss (B) and subordinates (S).

Power distance is a measure of the interpersonal power or influence between B and S as perceived by the least powerful of the two. As shown in table 4 there is a significant gap between Great Britain and Brazil in this dimension. Power distance dimension is linked with the inequality of societies regarding wealth and status among a country's overall population. It is used as a characteristic of social systems. For example, to explain the 'authoritarianism' of whole societies and their dominant supervision styles. According to this concept, Brazilian society tends to be more authoritarian than British society in terms of leadership styles. Brazilian managers enjoy the status differences between B and S. This cultural trait played an important role in the pace of culture change process in Usiminas. Managers resisted accepting modifications in the organizational structure when different roles and responsibilities were allocated and a flatter organization designed (step 6 of figure 1). This phenomenon, a high level of resistance in reshaping the organization structure, was less evident with British managers as shown in this research. This can be explained by the differences in power distance index between Brazil and Britain.

Table 4
Table 4
Power distance index (PDI)

Country	PDI Actual	PDI Predicted	Country	PDI Actual	PDI Predicted
Philippines	94	73	South Africa	49	62
Mexico	81	70	Argentina	49	56
Venezuela	81	66	USA	40	42
India	77	78	Canada	39	36
Singapore	74	64	Netherlands	38	38
Brazil	*69*	*72*	Australia	36	44
Hong Kong	68	56	Germany (FR)	35	42
France	68	42	*Great Britain*	*35*	*45*
Colombia	67	75	Switzerland	34	42
Turkey	66	60	Finland	33	30
Belgium	65	36	Norway	31	27
Peru	64	69	Sweden	31	23
Thailand	64	74	Ireland	28	37
Chile	63	56	New Zealand	22	35
Portugal	63	53	Denmark	18	28
Greece	60	51	Israel	13	44
Iran	58	61	Austria	11	40
Taiwan	58	63			
Spain	57	56	Mean of 39	51	52
Pakistan	55	74	countries		
Japan	54	57	(HERMES)		
Italy	50	53			

Actual values and values predicted on the basis of multiple regression
on latitude, population size, and wealth.

Adapted from Hofstede, 1980, p. 104

Individualism

Individualism is another dimension of national culture identified by Hofstede. It describes the relationship between the individual and collectively which prevails in a given society.

Individualism is reflected in the way people live together, for example, in their immediate families, 'extended families' or tribes. In the UK individualism is generally seen as a blessing and a source of well being; in Brazil it is certainly seen as alienating.

The human species is no doubt classified as a gregarious animal but different human societies show gregariousness to different degrees. See table 5.

Table 5
Country individualism index (IDV)

Country	IDV Actual	IDV Predicted	Country	IDV Actual	IDV Predicted
USA	91	95	Argentina	46	47
Australia	90	62	Iran	41	34
Great Britain	*89*	*74*	*Brazil*	*38*	*37*
Canada	80	80	Turkey	37	35
Netherlands	80	71	Greece	35	41
New Zealand	79	58	Philippines	32	23
Italy	76	62	Mexico	30	33
Belgium	75	71	Portugal	27	42
Denmark	74	75	Hong Kong	25	29
Sweden	71	85	Chile	23	38
France	71	80	Singapore	20	15
Ireland	70	52	Thailand	20	19
Norway	69	73	Taiwan	17	27
Switzerland	68	73	Peru	16	22
Germany (FR)	67	81	Pakistan	14	22
South Africa	65	38	Colombia	13	18
Finland	63	68	Venezuela	12	28
Austria	55	61			
Israel	54	47	Mean of 39	51	50
Spain	51	51	countries		
India	48	34	(HERMES)		
Japan	46	60			

Work goal scores were computed for a stratified sample of seven occupations at two points in time. Actual values and values predicted on the basis of multiple regression on wealth, latitude, and organization size.

Adapted from Hofstede, 1980, p. 222

According to Hofstede's studies, UK people tend to be more individualist, whereas Brazil has a more collectivist society. The impact of this cultural difference on the change process was clear: although all five firms considered employee participation vital for a smooth process of change, Brazilian employees responded more promptly to the team work activities and to participatory decision making training programmes. Brazilian people are eager to participate, work in groups, and be involved. In Britain, more intensive training courses were necessary to achieve similar results in terms of employee involvement programmes.

In summary, the context/content of a culture (i.e. national value system) can either represent a barrier or a facilitating factor when dealing with the process of organizational culture change. A better understanding of the cultural differences is a major contribution that the social sciences can make to practical policy matters (Hofstede, 1980). Nevertheless, the clear identification of what is common and what is specific in cross national comparisons seems to represent a great challenge to organizational theorists.

Conclusions

Because privatization programmes are under way in many countries, it is a timely moment to examine the implications of the structure of ownership for the behaviour and performance of firms. This book analyses how managerial behaviour and attitudes evolved as a result of new top management values.

Privatization, as a stimulus for culture change, involves a number of complex decisions at a strategic level (new core mission and organization structure) and at a detailed level (modifications in career management). Anticipation of these requirements and thorough planning of each step are, perhaps, the keys to a smooth and successful process of change.

The conclusions drawn from this study suggest that changing culture is a complex, long term undertaking that involves coordinated efforts by top leadership to change their own values/behaviour and the signals they send to others in the organization. Such changes must be reinforced by shifts in management processes such as: reward systems, management education, selection and promotion. To consider an organization as an interconnected living organism suggests that culture cannot be managed as something apart from the rest of the organization, as shown in this book - integrated actions are necessary.

The results of this research raise the question of whether the extensive changes which came as a result of privatization could have actually happened if these companies had remained nationalised. It seems that change in ownership did not necessarily bring organizational change directly. Rather, the increased competition, deregulation of the market and leaders' new values are the factors which trigger culture changes in the organization. Career management, although not responsible for provoking culture changes alone, is revealed as playing an important role in reinforcing new managerial attitudes and, consequently, gradually reshaping the corporate culture. By and large, managers are now being selected, promoted, trained and rewarded differently compared with before privatization. These modifications in career management reflect the changes in the way managers are expected to behave when major organizational changes occur.

As demonstrated by comparing the UK and Brazilian studies, there may be more universal issues in approaches to organization change than realized. One needs, however, to put the basic outline of a theory or approach in the cultural context relevant to the country. It is fundamental to be aware of both the similarities (universal dimensions, in this case, 'the processes') and the differences (specific dimensions, 'the context').

I found that British and Brazilian business situations contained specific cultural characteristics, such as how employees communicate with each other, with their customers and with superiors. However, both Brazilian and British managers provided similar diagnoses of and solutions to managerial and organizational problems related to corporate culture changes associated with their governments' privatization decisions. It seems that managerial issues and organizational process are becoming increasingly similar throughout the world.

The main contribution of the book is that it provides the reader (managers, consultants, researchers) with an integrative model of culture change within organizations: a universal approach. It explains how each step of the model is implemented. The model of culture change was devised based on the experience of firms in a country that has by far the greatest experience with this growing worldwide phenomenon. The model has been tested in a large Brazilian firm undergoing culture change associated with privatization decision. Through the case studies (Chapters 5, 6 and 7), this book provides management accounts of the main difficulties and barriers found during the transition phase, as well as the strategy suggested to minimise resistance.

Organizational change is a key issue facing managers today, especially with the drive to privatize many companies throughout the world. Studies of companies in Britain and Brazil have identified a common process which managers can use to drive organizational change more successfully, whether it is related to privatization or not.

9 Appendices 1, 2, and 3

Appendix 1

Introduction

This appendix explains the research strategy chosen to investigate the problem, that is the process of culture change within organizations. Additionally, it explores different theories regarding alternative ways of investigating organizations. Furthermore, included in this chapter are the theoretical assumptions which form the basis for the study.

The paradigm adopted in the present research is termed the 'interpretative'. The interpretative paradigm focuses on the notion that people enact their own reality either individually or in concert with others (Smircich, 1983). The study of organizational culture adopted here involves:

1   The assumption that reality is socially constructed.
2   The adoption of the interactionist position.
3   The qualitative type of evidence and the ethnographic tools.

Research strategy

> Life is a journey, not a destination (Mintzberg, 1979, p. 23).

In this section I will describe my journey into this research, looking back over the stream of decisions concerning this major study. In retrospect, some seem more deliberate to me (such as the case study approach), others more casually emergent (such as the data collection decisions), but in general they appear to represent a blending of the two. My research strategy, then, is formed by these strains.

The choice of a research strategy in social science is linked directly to assumptions about ontology, epistemology and human nature (Burrell and Morgan, 1982). For example, ontologically speaking, in the context of this investigation, the 'reality' to be investigated is not 'out there' as an objective nature, but it is a product of managers' perceptions. Following these assumptions, I also believe that knowledge is something which cannot be acquired, but something which has to be personally experienced. Regarding the relationship between human beings and their environment, I agree with Freire's (1976) position that people have an active and creative role in responding to environmental demands rather than a passive one. Consequently, when doing research we necessarily play a very active role. I believe that, as a result of this process, we become different persons. As has already been said by Burrell and Morgan (1982), we form and transform ourselves when investigating the world.

The way I look at social science, and consequently, how I developed this research was, basically, a process of interaction, or better still, of 'engagement'. It can be better illustrated by the following quotation:

> Scientists engage a subject of study by interacting with it by means of a particular frame of reference, and what is observed and discovered in the object is a product of this interaction (Burrell and Morgan, 1982, p. 13).

Burrell and Morgan (1982) also consider that in science it is possible to engage an object of study in different ways:

> ... we might engage an apple by looking at it, feeling it, or eating it (p. 35).

Hence, according to Burrell and Morgan (1982), the same object is capable of yielding many different kinds of knowledge. This leads me to see knowledge as a potentiality resting in an object of investigation and to see science as being concerned with the realisation of potentialities - of possible knowledge.

An understanding of research as engagement emphasises the importance of understanding the network of assumptions and practices that link the researcher to the phenomenon being investigated. For instance, it seems logical to say that my present assumptions are a result of my previous personal experience in working for large multinational and national organizations in Brazil, therefore a result of experiencing distinct corporate cultures. Furthermore, living in two countries of contrasting cultures, Brazil and England, reinforced my initial interest in cultural differences.

There are methodologies employed in social sciences, even in studies of careers and culture (see Driver and Coombs, 1983), which treat the social world like the natural world, as being hard, real and external to the individual.

132

As Glaser and Strauss (1967) have pointed out, they assume that a logic of hypothesis testing is the primary basis of scientific enquiry. While this may be appropriate to the kind of data processed in the natural sciences, social scientists researching organizations have to bear in mind that social variables are intrinsically more difficult to isolate and test (Morgan and Smircich, 1980). My view of this research is as being of a much softer, personal and more subjective quality.

The interactionist position adopted in this research is concerned with the creation and change of 'symbolic orders' via social interaction. For 'positivists', methods are mere data collection techniques (Morgan and Smircich, 1980). The interactionist is bound to view research itself as a symbolic order based on interactions. Interactionists are likely to define themselves in a subject to subject relation to their data, while positivists use an object-object model.

There are three basic premises underlying the interactive position:

1   That human beings act towards things on the basis of the meanings that the things have for them.

2   That the meaning of such things is derived from or arises out of the social interaction that one has with one's fellows.

3   That meanings are handled in, and modified through, an interpretative process used by the person dealing with the things she/he encounters (Blumer, 1969).

The qualitative type of evidence and the ethnographic tools

Historically, in the 1960s, around ninety per cent of the papers published in the two leading American sociology journals were based on quantitative survey research (Silverman, 1985). According to Silverman (1985), survey research was just as dominant in the UK during that period. The popularity of quantitative methods started to decline in sociology after 1965. While psychologists, economists, clinicians and administrators were still inclined to discount any research not based on counting, sociologists after this date tended to feel rather awkward about being seen, for instance, carrying out a statistical test of significance (Silverman, 1985).

Today, however, the picture is very different. There is widespread recognition that the research traditions based on measurement of organization variables may fail to describe realities as they are experienced by organizational actors (Tichy, 1982). Methods derived from the natural sciences have come to be seen as increasingly unsatisfactory as a basis for social research (Morgan and Smircich, 1980).

The ethnographic tools An ethnographic approach involves a wide range of observational techniques and interviews using an interactive position. This approach focuses on three fundamental aspects of human experience: what people do, what they know and how they think. When all of these are learned and shared, they become cultural knowledge. The essence of an ethnography is 'thick description' - an analysis of culture, not as experimental science in search of laws, but as an interpretative one in search of meaning (Ellen, 1984). The end result of an ethnographic research project is the interpretation and understanding of the meaning of systems of those individuals under study.

In this research, the case studies stem from a comparative framework. Therefore, they are based on relatively short periods of contact. This represents a limitation when viewed from the ethnographic perspective.

The main difference between the ethnographic tools and those used by functionalists is that in the functionalist interview, the researcher distances him/herself from daily organizational life, removing him/herself from active involvement in the organization or phenomenon under investigation. It is a rational approach, which emphasises the measurable social facts and formal structure of the organization.

The theoretical framework

Beginning with Glaser and Strauss (1967), much has been written about developing 'grounded theory', being open to what the site has to tell us, and slowly evolving a coherent framework rather than 'imposing' one from the start. However, the need to develop grounded theory usually exists in opposition with the need for clarity and focus:

> Research projects that pretend to come to the study with no assumptions usually encounter much difficulty (Miles, 1979, p. 15).

All researchers make choices. In making those choices none of them starts with his mind a blank waiting for it to be filled with evidence. Our training, experiences and predilections influence our preferred research strategies. I adopted Miles (1979) approach to theoretical conceptualization when planning my research. He believes that a rough working frame needs to be in place near the beginning of field work. Of course, it will change. Thus, I chose the strategy of developing explicit preliminary frameworks quite early; even so, I revised them repeatedly throughout the life of the project. The main revision, however, occurred after the pilot study data analysis.

134

The pilot study indicated the need to adjust the methodological approach used in the following case studies.

1   In Jaguar I studied: the 'prevailing culture' and the 'appropriate culture' (perceived as the 'ideal way of doing things' by top management).

2   In BNFL, BA, BAA and Usiminas the case studies are composed of: historical culture, prevailing (current) culture, appropriate culture.

As shown in figure 20, I expected that in analysing companies during their processes of change it might be easier to spot how managerial careers change as a reflection of culture change. Consequently, I would be able to show the impact of culture on careers at two moments: before a major culture change (situation A) and during a major culture change (situation B).

To understand how culture is changed it is important, first, to understand how culture is created. Therefore, the theoretical framework includes the investigation of the founder's and the industry's values.

Although these three components seem to overlap emphasis was placed on the historical and prevailing cultures in order to avoid a 'futuristic' hypothetical approach.

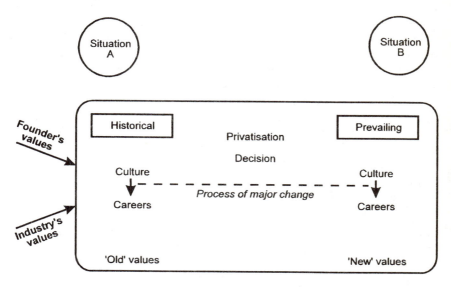

Figure 20 Theoretical framework (b)

135

The 'processual' perspective Adopting Pettigrew's (1988) perspective, I used a 'processual' analysis, in that an organization or any other social system may profitably be explored as a continuous system, with a past, a present and a future. Organizations shift in response to market, environmental or social forces. These shifts are hard to detect when they occur, but they are easy to recognise in retrospect through each organization's passages and history. Learning to identify these events was part of my task as researcher.

This research, thus, must take into account the history and future of a system and relate them to the present. The process itself, as explained by Pettigrew (1988), is seen as a continuous interdependent sequence of actions and events that can be used to explain the origins, continuation, and outcome of some phenomenon. The focus is as much on the process of 'becoming' as on that of 'being'.

Using the 'processual' approach could also facilitate the emergence of other issues, such as the links between organizational change and human resource management. As Pettigrew (1988) says, business change has been a significant driving force for human resource change. By using the variable of change, I could enrich the findings of this research by analysing how human resource management copes with changes in the organization as a whole. As mentioned by Pettigrew (1988), much attention has been devoted to the outcomes of organizational change while comparatively little has been given to the way such changes are managed.

Silverman (1985), has also mentioned the importance of studying organizations as continuous systems when he writes about 'chronology' in research. According to him, in many research areas analysing data over time gives an additional perspective. He considers that, over time, we can seek to understand the dynamics of social relations.

This study uses a time dimension. I assumed that to understand organizational culture change it would be necessary to investigate the historical and also the current corporate set of values, beliefs and assumptions. This idea is illustrated by the following quotation:

> Understanding organizational cultures and how they are maintained and transferred over time is not always apparent to anyone taking only a horizontal slice from the organizational life (Davies and Easterby-Smith, 1985, p. 28)

As implied by Davis and Easterby-Smith (1985), the process of change can be identified and studied only against a background of structure or relative constancy.

As Pettigrew (1988) puts it, social realities depend, to a great extent, on the nature and development of a 'figure/ground' relationship. In other words, elements in a potentially vast perceptual field are differentiated from their wider context and interpreted through a frame of reference that provides the basis for a coherent organization of perception and experience (Morgan and Smircich, 1980).

Periods of culture change under investigation Pettigrew (1979) considers that any study on change must cover a specific period of time. He also emphasises that one of the first steps in this type of research is actually to identify what period the investigation is covering. In this particular research, I decided to study periods around the privatization process as I assumed that it would coincide with major changes. Therefore, as the privatization occurred at different times in different firms, the periods under investigation vary from firm to firm.

Periods which preceded privatization were when the major changes occurred. This was concluded after my primary case study - Jaguar. Therefore, this research concentrated on analysing changes during the period of post privatization for Jaguar, and both pre and post privatization for British Nuclear Fuels (BNFL), British Airways (BA), British Airports Authority (BAA) and Usiminas.

In order to analyse and compare two different periods in each organization (before and during the privatization process), I specified two periods of investigation - the 'historical' and 'prevailing' periods - in each organization, as shown in figure 21.

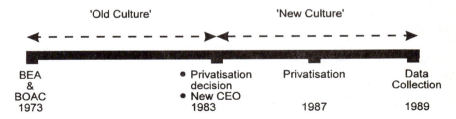

Figure 21 Periods under investigation (example of BA)

It is important to note that the 'prevailing period', when major changes started to occur, coincides with the privatization decision and the appointment of a CEO in each organization.

a) Historical period A retrospective approach was considered appropriate as I am interested in the present managers' perceptions of the past. What actually happened in the past is not really the issue in this research. Rather, I am interested in investigating how managers, as a group, perceive the historical events and how this contributes to their better understanding of their own organizations.

137

b) Prevailing period This is considered to start when top management launched programmes to prepare the organization for privatization. Coincidentally, those periods were initiated when new chief executive officers (CEOs) were appointed to help the organizations in their adaptation process in a different economic environment. The way I actually identify these periods in each company is best explained in each case study chapter. By selecting the periods of organizational change under study, it becomes clear that this research investigates, mainly, the process of discontinuous change, i.e. a major change triggered by external environmental pressures. For the purpose of this research, the process of privatization is considered as a political action potentially affecting the economic environment within which the organizations operate.

Tichy (1982), studying discontinuous change, points out that organizations nowadays are facing increasingly turbulent, and often hostile, environments.

> Now we are moving into the era of discontinuous change brought on by energy problems, finite resource limits, the limits of the environment in the absorption of industrial wastes. This accelerating rate of change in the business world is, in some ways, provoking a faster rate of change within organizations, specifically in the way managers are expected to behave (p. 58).

This approach contrasts with studies which have been done on continuous change. See, for example, Schein 1985b, Pettigrew (1985) and Dyer (1980). They tend to analyse organizational change as part of the gradual 'evolution' process of an organization. The present study focuses on a 'revolution' period provoked by a discontinuity in the external economic environment.

Formulating research questions

It was a direct step from elaboration of a conceptual framework to the formulation of my main research questions. The former set up the latter. As shown below, my main research questions are a reflection of the framework (see figure 20).

Research questions:

a) How does corporate culture influence managerial careers?
     - before a major change
     - after a major change

b) How does privatization instigate culture change?

138

The emphasis on how instead of why is a relevant issue which differentiates the research questions in a functionalist paradigm from those in an interpretative paradigm.

The research questions represented a way of making my theoretical assumptions even more explicit than they may have been in the contextual framework. Furthermore, they told me what I want to know *most*. It helped to channel energy in this direction rather than in the direction of other variables and relationships. My collection of data, thus, was more directly focused.

In an interpretative paradigm, research questions are not rigid. They are revised after each case study, i.e. other issues emerge from the data and are incorporated with the initial research questions. In this present research the following questions came out during the data collection and analysis:

a) The 'need' for a culture change (an analysis of the environment constraint).
b) The organizational mission (before and after a 'major change').
c) The steps companies utilised in their process of culture change.
d) The role of managerial careers in the culture change process.

The case study approach

According to Yin (1981a), the use of case studies is appropriate whenever:

- An empirical inquiry claims to examine a contemporary phenomenon in its real life context, especially when

- The boundaries between the phenomenon and its context are not clearly evident.

In contrast, other research strategies have other strengths. An experiment, for instance, deliberately divorces a phenomenon from its context, so that attention can be focused on a few variables. Each strategy is best suited to a different set of conditions, and each strategy is therefore likely to be favoured whenever such conditions prevail.

Although the peculiar strength of the case study is its ability to cover both a contemporary phenomenon and its context, this characteristic also creates a special difficulty: once the context has been incorporated into a study, the number of variables of interest will inevitably be greater than the number of data points (i.e. the number of cases). This means that few, if any, statistics will be relevant for analysing the data.

I decided to use the case study approach in my research as a consequence of:

a) my own previous experience when developing a single qualitative case study during my MSc dissertation (1980). I learned through this experience that the case study allows the researcher to enter in depth the process of understanding organizational problems.

b) establishing the type of research questions best addressed to the essential problem being studied. I considered that a case study would be the appropriate method to analyse the process by which corporate culture impinges on managerial careers.

In case studies, the context is part of the study. My research questions and consequently my interview schedule (see appendices 2 and 3) imply a deep investigation involving 'figure ground'. For example, I formulated questions such as: 'What type of manager gets on in this particular organization?' Describe the 'deviant manager' in this same context. But, if an organization is in the process of change, what is deviant today is not necessarily deviant tomorrow.

If cultural elements interact closely (as shown in Chapter 4), a comprehensive approach to analysing organizational cultures would yield better results than studying isolated cultural elements. An example of the latter is the study by Driver and Coombs (1983). They studied how reward incentives should be flexible to fit different employees and values. They studied reward incentives in an isolated way, dissociated from any other aspects of rewards (such as promotion) or even appraisal. Trice and Beyer (1984) also reinforce this idea:

> Cultural elements tend to be very intimately associated and influence one another (p. 653).

Morgan and Smircich (1980) adopt Yin's (1981a) ideas which I described earlier. They point out that, as a research strategy, the distinguishing characteristic of the case study is that the boundaries between phenomenon and context are not clearly evident.

Although major improvements in case study research are still to be made, Yin (1981b) considers that case studies could be used as a 'systematic research tool' (1981b). Case studies can be done by using either qualitative or quantitative evidence. The evidence may come from field work interviews, archival records, verbal reports, observations or any combination of these. Nor does the case study imply the use of a particular data collection method. A common misconception is that case studies are solely the result of ethnographic studies, or of participant observation. Conversely, according to Yin, using these methods does not always lead to the production of case studies.

140

The four sites chosen were: Jaguar Cars, British Nuclear Fuels, British Airways and British Airports Authority. The selection of research 'sites' (the term used by Miles, 1979, meaning, in this context, 'companies') was shaped by the choice of the research questions being posed. As described before, I was interested in investigating how careers and culture relate to each other in firms experiencing 'major' culture change process.

This study was conducted over a period of eighteen months from July 1988 to December 1989 at four large British organizations. I chose large organizations to ensure they had structured managerial career systems. The main common characteristic of these companies was that they were passing through major periods of change.

The research used five case studies and a qualitative type of evidence in order to pursue the answers to the research questions. It concentrated first on British companies which are passing through the processes of privatization. Furthermore, the same method was applied to investigate the process of culture change experienced by Usiminas in Brazil.

As explained in Chapter 2, it is claimed that privatization increases efficiency by provoking organizational change and emphasizing a more entrepreneurial style of management. I expected that the process of privatization would be a major factor in instigating culture change. During the preliminary interview to obtain access I investigated if in fact the organization had been passing through major changes.

a) Why these five case studies? There is an intentional or design component in the process of choosing and gaining access to particular organizations. This process can best be described, according to Pettigrew (1988) as 'planned opportunism'. It is with this expression in mind, that an exploratory survey was undertaken using secondary source data, i.e. newspapers and company reports, to identify particular organizations undergoing a process of major transition.

Having identified a small sample of suitable UK organizations, their human resources managers were initially contacted by telephone and subsequently in writing. At the preliminary interview, subjects discussed included logistics of the research, data collection method, and confidentiality of the data.

After a few false starts (for example, British American Tobacco - BAT), Jaguar Cars expressed a keen interest in the project. Without questioning their motives for participation, the opportunity to pilot the research was grasped! With hindsight, these motives were clearly a reflection of the organization's culture; namely to promote and improve the company image both publicly and with the academic community.

141

The other organizations studied: 1) British Nuclear Fuels Limited (BNFL)
Why did I choose British Nuclear Fuels Limited (BNFL)? The choice of the subsequent organizations studied was influenced by the acceptance of Jaguar, and hence the necessity to find a common link. One of the principal findings from the pilot study of Jaguar Cars was the need to change the organizational culture as the company was transformed from being a government owned to a publicly quoted company. As perceived by managers, the prevailing culture for a nationalised organization was clearly inappropriate for a recently privatized company, now responsible to its shareholders rather than to bureaucrats.

Therefore (an insight which came during the data analysis of Jaguar), managers believe that privatization requires a culture change. Through the press (Fishlock, 1986), I realized that BNFL was experiencing a major transformation. This change was a consequence of different factors which included its preparation for privatization. Having read this, I contacted the Human Resources Director.

BNFL likewise proved receptive to my proposal. Again the reasons could be linked to their culture. Traditionally, the organization was very secretive; this aptly reflects the political sensitivity of the industry. A component of the strategy for culture change includes a need to be more open and co-operative with the public and local community.

2) British Airways (BA) The main reason for the choice of BA as my third case study was that the criteria should match the first two previous case studies namely: a) UK company; b) passing through a process of major change as a consequence, mainly, of privatization.

Access initially proved to be difficult with the Human Resources Manager showing great resistance. This seemed to stem from his sceptical opinion of academia. He finally consented in the hope of obtaining the results of the other case studies.

3) British Airports Authority (BAA) The criteria chosen to select BAA were identical to those for BA. The organization proved to be extremely supportive throughout the research process, not only at the initial meeting, but during data collection and interviewing. This clearly reflects co-operatives, participating style and the desire to present to the 'outside world' the way they have successfully transformed the organization. These BAA traits of culture are fully described in Chapter 5.

4) Usiminas The rationale to study Usiminas (a Brazilian steel organization) was primarily to test whether the integrative model of culture change (see figure 1) would apply to explain the cultural transition experienced by a Brazilian organization.

Interviews were used to collect the majority of data. Additional information was gathered through annual reports, company's history and company's specific documents such as (mission statements, personnel forms, management development philosophy).

Following my original framework (see figure 20), two main areas of investigation were covered: corporate culture and managerial career systems. I formulated separate questions to explore each of these two themes (see appendices 2 and 3). Additionally, at the end of interviews, I asked about the managers' own perceptions on the impact of culture on careers. For some of them, these links were clear, for others, it was really a 'difficult question'.

a) Data collection regarding corporate culture   Schein (1985a) considers that there are three different perspectives on investigating culture:

*   Historical - based on understanding the organization's specific antecedents, it assumes that every culture is unique.

*   Evolutionistic - it assumes that every culture goes through a predictable and directional process toward ever higher stages, and

*   Ecological - which assumes that culture can be explained only by the adaptive functions that its various elements fulfil.

I believe that these are not competing but complementary points of view, each of which is needed for a full understanding of the observed phenomena. My approach in this research is predominantly a mixture of the three as I investigated the unique history of each organization, how it developed and also the environmental changes that triggered culture change.

As observed by Fitzgerald (1988), a central difficulty in deciphering corporate culture is that values and assumptions resist the usual forms of investigation. Some authors believe in measuring company values (see for example, Mattsson (1985) and his axiological method for measuring company's values). However, as observed by Fitzgerald (1988), the typical tools of conventional research - classification and measurement - do not work well in this realm because values do not exist as isolated, independent or incremental entities.

> Beliefs and assumptions, tastes and inclinations, hopes and purposes, values and principles are not modular packages stored on warehouse shelves, waiting for inventory. They have no separate existence, as do spark plugs in an engine. They cannot be

examined one at a time and replaced when burned out. Usually they are not readily disposable, cast off as one changes a soiled shirt... (p. 12).

Organizational culture researchers have done no better than the anthropologists in developing a universal acceptable methodological approach to the study of culture (Martin and Meyerson, 1988). Different researchers actually study formal and informal organizational practices (see Gunz, 1989) as cultural manifestations. However, as pointed out by Martin and Meyerson (1988), to study only practices is to risk being guilty of 'selling old wine in new skins'. Anthropologists, in particular ethnomethodologists, for instance, emphasise the importance of studying the jargon and special language, humour and physical arrangements such as office or dress codes (see Martin & Meyerson, 1988). They are not concerned with what people think (their concepts) but with what they do. Schein (1984a) goes deeper in the study of culture. He focuses on the study of values, beliefs and assumptions. The latter is the approach adopted in the present research on studying organizational culture.

The study of culture is not an objective or distanced observation of a reified object. It is enacted, not observed. Researchers and cultural members enact what they perceive and fail to enact what they fail to perceive. Furthermore, cultural members and researchers may be unconscious or preconscious of some aspects of culture that have been repressed, simply forgotten, or taken for granted. This idea is better illustrated by Kroeber and Kluckhohn's (1952) statement:

It would hardly be the fish who discovered the existence of water (p. 48).

Thus, in this research, cultural paradigms are considered as a subjective point of view that determines what a person perceives, conceives and enacts. This approach is based on Schein's (1985b) recommendation and differs from Silverman's (1985) point of view. Silverman (1985) embraces the realistic approach. He prefers to use observation to get data that is 'untouched by human hands'. Similarly, Mintzberg (1979) uses 'direct research' in observing a manager in his own working setting and in doing his normal daily job.

The interpretative approach seems to be more appropriate to investigate culture than the realistic as it tries to decipher the unconscious level of culture (the values, assumptions) instead of analysing only 'the observable dimensions of a phenomenon under study'. Because the values, beliefs and assumptions are invisible and only discovered by 'challenging' or 'probing', they cannot be investigated by using a superficial observation method.

The levels of culture the study tries to decipher and analyse is based on Schein's classification as shown in figure 22.

Artifacts and creations The most visible level of the culture is its artifacts and creations - its constructed physical and social environment. At this level, one can look at physical space, the technological output of the group, its written and spoken language, its artistic productions and the overt behaviour of its members. If one wants to achieve this level of understanding more quickly, one can attempt to analyse the central values that provide the day to day operating principles by which the members of the culture guide their behaviour.

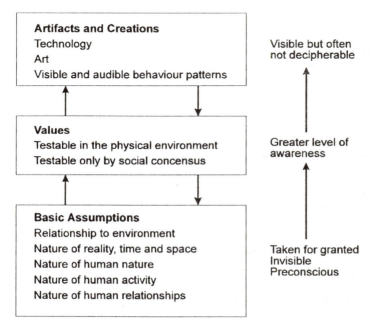

Source: Adapted from Schein, 1985a, p4.

Figure 22 Levels of culture

Values According to Schein (1984a), 'Values reflect what ought to be, as distinct from what is' (p. 12). He explains how values are created in a group; for instance, when a group faces a new task, issue or problem, the first solution proposed to deal with it can only have the status of a value because there is not as yet a shared basis for determining what is factual and real. Someone in the group, usually the founder, has convictions about the nature of the problem (in effect, the nature of reality) and how to deal with it, and will propose a solution based on those convictions. That individual may

145

regard the proposed solution as a belief or principle based on facts, but the group cannot feel that same degree of conviction until it has collectively shared in successful problem solution. For example, in a young business if sales begin to decline, the leader may say, 'We must increase advertising', because of his belief that 'advertising always increases sales'. The group, never having experienced this situation before, will hear that assertion as a statement of the leaders' values: 'He thinks that one should always advertise more when one is in trouble'. What the leader initially proposes, therefore, cannot have any status other than as a value to be questioned, debated, and challenged.

Basic assumptions When a solution to a problem works repeatedly, it comes to be taken for granted. We come to believe that nature really works this way. In fact, if a basic assumption is strongly held in a group, members would find behaviour based on any other premise inconceivable. It seems that assumptions actually guide behaviour.

According to Schein (1985a), there is no quick way to identify these cultural attributes of an organization. Culture does not reveal itself easily. The approach proposed by Schein (1985a) to uncover values and assumptions is described by him as an interactive 'clinical' interview, a series of encounters and joint explorations between the investigator and various motivated informants who live in the organization and embody its culture. The main assumption of this approach is that only a joint effort between an outsider and an insider can decipher the essential cultural assumptions and their pattern of interrelationships (Schein, 1984a).

Questions formulated regarding corporate culture A warming up question was about the managers' perceptions of the personality of the organization as if it were a person. I also asked how this personality had changed over the years. The idea of using the metaphor of organization as personality in order to decipher the 'taken for granted' values, beliefs and assumptions, is my adaptation of Morgan's (1986) theoretical views on the process of understanding organizations. Additionally, I investigated the founders' and past leaders' main values and beliefs as well as current leaders' main values and beliefs. The patterns of behaviour which characterize managers from different types of industry (car manufacturing, nuclear, airline, airport) were also investigated. I posed special questions regarding the external environmental constraints both in the past and at the time of the investigation in order to understand the need for a culture change.

b) Data collected regarding managerial careers The study of careers, from an organizational perspective, has been traditionally focused on an objective methodological approach (see, for example, Gunz (1989) in his study of 'climbing frames'). In this research, although I gathered some formal data from personnel officers regarding career systems practices, the main approach relies on managers' perceptions of managerial careers within the organizations under study. The data relating to managerial careers focused explicitly on the managerial profile that the organization searches for when it selects executives and what managerial profile the organization reinforces when it promotes executives by upgrading them on the career ladder. The management training and development, appraisal and reward were investigated as well. Because I intended to probe, many questions were considered by the interviewees as 'difficult', 'interesting', or 'I have never thought about this before, but it is fascinating'... I was trying to understand, to catch, their view of the social world they live in. In this task, listening was important, as I was engaging in dialogue, using questions such as: 'Could you explain better?' or 'What do you mean by that?'

Questions formulated regarding managerial careers   I asked about the expected managerial behaviour (both historical, and as it has been changing over the years). Questions such as 'who gets on?', and 'who is deviant?', were very helpful in deciphering each firm's expected managerial behaviour over the years. Furthermore, I asked questions regarding:

*   the criteria the organizations use to select managers
*   the criteria the organizations use to appraise, promote and reward managers
*   the contents and directions of management training and development programmes

c)   The sample of managers in each company   Altogether a total of eighty two interviews were conducted between August 1988 and March 1992 covering the five case studies. Semi structured interviews were conducted with: a) personnel managers, b) line managers, and c) personnel directors. The line managers were taken from different areas of the organization. In terms of seniority, they ranged from middle to senior managers, who had been employed by the company for at least five years. It was felt that such managers would possess the relevant experience within the company necessary to document the process of change. I chose to study culture through this upper level because, influenced by Van Maanen (1983), I believe that the corporate values held by management are reflected in behaviour throughout an organization.

In the light of practical opportunism, it proved necessary to interview five managers (out of a sample of eighty two) who had been employed by the

147

company for less than two years. In all cases, the interviewees were contacted by telephone by their respective human resources departments. Participation in the study was purely optional, being at the discretion of the individual concerned. In Jaguar, however, attendance at the interview was compulsory. Therefore the interviewees felt obliged to participate and regarded the whole process as an imposition. Clearly this required careful handling to overcome their initial prejudices and reflects the 'authoritarian' type of culture as described by managers I interviewed. In one instance, a manager actually refused to attend the pre arranged meeting.

The data analysis method

The most serious and central difficulty in the use of qualitative data is that methods of analysis are not well formulated (Miles, 1979). For quantitative data, there are clear conventions the researcher can use. When faced with a bank of qualitative data, I had very few guidelines for protection against self delusion. The initial framework, however, was useful to help me in this analysis.

My approach in data analysis stressed the very active role people play in enacting their organizational reality and in developing shared interpretations for their experience.

a) Analysis during data collection Conducting partial analysis during data collection allowed me to move back and forth between thinking about the existing data and generating strategies for collecting new data; for example, usually I found out that I needed to interview specific people. On some occasions I felt the need to talk to people at lower levels of the organization (to get more detailed data about the day to day routine of career systems, for example) or sometimes at higher levels when I needed to get data on the environmental constraints influencing culture change. It seemed to me a cyclical activity - getting data and analysing data.

b)   Within site analysis   This research used the method of drawing conclusions about every single site. It is focused on description, analysis and explanation of what occurred in each single case study. The idea was to make an effort to merge with a well grounded sense of the local reality in a particular setting. This method of analysis was chosen as it is consistent with the research questions, i.e. the main issue of this study is to show the relationship between careers and culture within a specific organization. Furthermore, a cross analysis was accomplished. Below, I explain how I analysed the data of pilot study.

c) Data analysis in the pilot study: Jaguar The method I used to analyse the data collected in Jaguar differed from the one I used for the three remaining companies. In Jaguar, I listened to the tapes in order to interpret the contents of answers. The notes I wrote during the interviews were also utilised in this process of data analysis. I did not transcribe all the tapes, as, at that stage, I did not realise how important this step was. Hence, in contrast to the other three case studies, I relied on my notes and my interpretations in listening (several times) to the tapes to build a picture of how careers relate to culture in Jaguar. A report was produced, linking the findings with the literature, and sent to the organization to be validated.

d) Data analysis in BNFL, BA, BAA and Usiminas Each case study was analysed immediately after I finished the data collection. When all of them were analysed, then a cross case analysis was produced. Nearly 200 pages of tape transcriptions were produced from the BNFL, BA and BAA case studies. The process of transcription was not a mechanical one. Listening and transcribing tapes was very useful in my process of understanding the content. When all the transcriptions were produced, in each case study, I read them in order to find consensus among managers. When I could not find consensus, I reported it and tried to understand why. I put numbers (from 1 to 5) to identify the answers relating to the interview schedule (1 - historical culture; 2 - prevailing culture; 3 - need for a change; 4 - historical careers; 5 - prevailing careers). Then, I put together all answers regarding the five main themes. To produce the report, I chose the most significant quotations to represent consensus when it was achieved. This process of analysis was time consuming and painful. It took seven hours on average to transcribe each one and half hour interview. The data analysis required four drafts for each case study until I got a final report. The first draft consisted of raw data, i.e. all managers' answers in each company to each question. In the second draft, I put all answers to each question together until I got fifteen answers to each question in the same block.

The chapters on BNFL, BA and BAA mainly focus on the data analysis, discussion and the results. In order to avoid repetitive issues, the links with the literature are mainly explained in Chapter 6, the cross case analysis.

e) Cross case analysis I used cross case analysis to find out similarities and differences among findings. By doing this, I expected to enrich, but not exhaust, my understanding of the problem at hand. Miles (1979) considers that in doing cross case studies, there is much potential for both greater explanatory power and greater generalisation than a single case study can deliver. It does not necessarily represent the reason why I chose the multiple case study approach. I believe that a single case study can have more potential for an even deeper investigation of the problem.

f) Validation Silverman (1985) says that a method of validation in the natural sciences is a replication of an initial experiment by a second investigator. Since such experimental settings are rare in social science, a common claim made by sociologists of an interpretative bent is that an analysis can be validated by the very members described. This is done by demonstrating a correspondence between the investigator's description and the description of members of the collectivity that is being investigated. While naturalists consider that 'members' pronouncements on findings cannot be treated as a test of validity', that is the way interpretists use to validate their data. An ethnomethodological approach seeks consensus among analysts (Silverman, 1985) because they mainly use observation techniques to analyse phenomena. I seek consensus among respondents to understand their own perception of corporate culture and its links with managerial careers.

In my research, a report was prepared with the analysis of each case study. This report was given to each company's key informant and followed up with a feedback interview. This approach was extremely useful in validating my findings. It provided an opportunity to enrich my original data with more information, or even slightly change my original interpretation. No major modification was necessary after these contacts. An interesting thing, however, occurred with the Jaguar case study. One of the key informants who read the report, considered it 'too negative'. He said:

> Everything in it is true, and I am surprised you caught all these in your research interviews. However, we prefer to keep the data confidential or change its tune.

This fact can be associated with their culture as selling a good image of the company. In other words, revealing some weakness in their change process could be perceived as negative from a commercial point of view.

Concluding remarks on methodology

I have collected the perceptions of individuals about how their companies operate. They were not asked whether or not they were satisfied with aspects of their job environments or whether their expectations about the organization were being met. Rather, their perceptions of how their company functions reflect the value systems or cultures of these companies as seen through management's eyes.

The interpretative paradigm sharply contrasts with the functionalist one. Some of the differences are as follows: Rather than studying people within organizations as functionalists do, interpretative approach means learning with people. Learning with people implies that the use of labels is avoided and researchers tend to utilise the language of informants to analyse their reality.

Advocates of the functionalist paradigm believe in the possibility of an objective and value free social science in which the scientist is distanced from the scene which he/she is analysing. The researcher's role is to develop the categories and rigid hypotheses which guide the investigation. It is the researcher who elaborates the scientific laws of the phenomena under study and develops categories and classifications which are postulated to govern the cause-effect relations between the variables of interest. The researcher distances him/herself from daily organizational life, removing him/herself from active involvement in the organization or phenomena under investigation. Traditional research methods are used in the functionalist paradigm, relying on the four customary means: adhering to scientific protocol, engaging in replication, testing hypotheses, and using operational procedures to analyse the phenomena of interest. The use of such operational procedures implies an ordered, structured, controlled and static view of the world.

The interpretative researcher does not have a specific goal in conducting the research, but only the general goal of discovering the knowledge that participants are using to organize their behaviour and interpret their experience. Attempts are made to use the language of the informants and the informants direct the investigator toward the important aspects of the informants' world. Research questions develop over time, after exposure to various aspects of the participants' culture.

Whereas the functionalist approach is linear and focused, the interpretative acts within a broad general context and it is only through the collection and analysis and further collection of ethnographic data that the initial research questions are revised and new questions emerge from the data collected.

Observations regarding the data gathered

As new facts are constantly appearing about these many enterprises and as some of the companies studied are currently undergoing organizational changes, I have arbitrarily set times in each organization as the cut off date for this investigation. Therefore, for the companies described here, I have not used information which appeared after these dates.

Appendix 2

Interview schedule utilised in the pilot study (Jaguar Cars).

Exploring prevailing corporate culture

* Describe the 'personality' of this organization.

* Talk about the history: growing up process; main difficulties in the past; founder's and leaders' values and their influence on organization's formal and informal rules.

The need for a change

* Describe the external demands: past and current ones.

What culture is appropriate for the company in the future?

* Who 'gets on' and 'who is deviant' today? Are these profiles changing?

Exploring managerial careers

* Career paths and speed, criteria for lateral and upward move.

* Are career systems reinforcing the prevailing or the appropriate culture?

Appendix 3

Interview schedule utilised in BNFL, BA, BAA and Usiminas.

Personal data

* How long have you been working for this firm?
* Current job?

The need for a change

* Environment constraints: before and after 'major change'.
* When should 'major' organizational changes start?

Describe the personality of this organization

* Before 'major' change: mission and past leaders' values.
* Now: mission and current leaders' values.

Exploring management style

* Who 'got on' yesterday? Who 'gets on' today?
* Who was 'deviant' yesterday? Who is 'deviant' today?

Exploring managerial career systems

* before major changes: * now:

   a) management selection   a) management selection
   b) management development   b) management development
   c) management appraisal   c) management appraisal
   d) management promotion   d) management promotion

In what way can managerial career systems help the organization to modify its corporate culture?

Bibliography

Adler, N.J. (1983), 'Cross Cultural Management Research: The Ostrich and the Trend', *Academy of Management Review*, vol. 8, no. 2, pp. 226-32.

Adler, N.J. and Jelinek, M. (1986), 'Is "Organisational Culture" Culture Bound?', *Human Resources Management*, vol. 25, no. 1, pp. 73-90.

Albert, M. (1985), 'Cultural Development Through Human Resource Systems Integration', *Training and Development Journal*, vol. 39, no. 9, pp. 76-81.

Allaire, Y. and Firsirotu, M.E. (1984), 'Theories of Organisational Culture', *Organisational Studies*, vol. 5, no. 3, pp. 193-226.

Amado, G., Faucheux, C. and Laurent, A. (1990), 'Organizational Change and Cultural Realities: Franco-American Contrasts', *L'Individu dans L'Organisation: Les Dimensions Oubliés*, Press de L'Université Laval, Québec.

Angle, H.L., Manz, C. and Van de Ven, A.H. (1985), 'Integrating Human Resource Management and Corporate Strategy: A Preview of the 3M Story', *Human Resources Management*, vol. 24, no. 1, pp. 51-68.

Archer, S. (1988), 'Qualitative Research and the Epistemological Problems of the Management Disciplines', in Pettigrew, A.M. (ed.), *Competitiveness and the Management Process*, Basil Blackwell, London.

Ashton, D. and Easterby-Smith, M. (1979), *Management Development in the Organisation*, Macmillan, London.

Becker, H.S., Greer, B., Hughes, E. and Straus, A. (1961), *Boys in White*, Chicago University Press, Chicago.

Boeker, W. (1989), 'Strategic Change: The Effects of Founding and History' *Academy of Management Journal*, vol. 32, no. 5, pp. 489-515.

Boscheck, R. (1994), 'Regulating European Electricity Supply: Issues and Implications', *Long Range Planning*, vol. 27, no. 5, pp. 111-23.

Brooks, I. and Bate, P. (1994), 'The Problems of Effecting Change Within The British Civil Service: A Cultural Perspective', *British Journal of Management*, vol. 5, pp. 177-90.

Brown, A. and Payne, R. (1990), 'A Human Resource Approach to the Management of Organisational Culture', Working Paper 200, Manchester Business School, U.K.

Bruce, M. (1987), 'Managing People First: Bringing the Service Concept to B.A.', *Industrial and Commercial Training*, pp. 21-6, March/April.

Bruce, M. and Moult, G. (1988), 'Moving into the Mainstream', *Management Education and Development*, vol. 19, no. 3, pp. 187-200.

Brus, W. and Lasky, M. (1989), *From Marx to Markets: Socialism in Service of an Economic System*, Clarendon Press, Oxford.

Bulmer, H. (1969), *Symbolic Interactionism: Perspective and Method*, Prentice-Hall, N.J.

Burgoyne, J.G. (1988), 'Management Development for the Individual and the Organisation', *Personnel Management*, vol. 20, no. 6, pp. 40-4, June.

Burgoyne, J.G. (1989), 'Creating the Managerial Portfolio: Building on Competency Approaches to Management Development', *Management Education and Development*, vol. 20, no. 1, pp. 56-61.

Burrell, G. and Morgan, G. (1982), *Sociological Paradigms and Organisational Analysis*, Gower Press, London.

Campbell, R.J. and Moses, J.L. (1985), 'Careers from an Organisational Perspective' in Hall, D.T. (ed.), *Career Development in Organisations*, Doubleday, New York.

Cardoso, E.A. (1991), 'Privatisation Fever in Latin America', *Challenge*, vol. 34, no. 5, pp. 35-41.

Chandler, A.D. (1962), *Strategy and Structure: Chapters in the History of the Industrial Enterprise*, MIT Press, Cambridge, Mass.

Child, J. (1972), 'Organisational Structure, Environment and Performance: The Role of Strategic Choice', *Sociology*, vol. 6, no. 1, pp. 1-21.

Child, J. (1981), 'Culture, Contingency and Capitalism in the Cross National Study of Organizations' in Cummings, L.L. and Straw, B.M. (eds.), *Research in Organisational Behaviour*, vol. 3, JAI Press Inc, Greenwich, Connecticut.

Colling, T. and Ferner, A. (1992), 'The Limits of Autonomy: Devolution, Line Managers and Industrial Relations in Privatized Companies', *Journal of Management Studies*, vol. 29, no. 2, pp. 209-27, March.

Comte, T.E. and McCanna, W.F. (1988), 'Progressive Differentiation: Improving the Strategic Act of CEO Selection', *Academy of Management Executive*, vol. II, no. 4, pp. 303-09.

Cook, P. and Kaptinck, C. (1988), *Privatization in Less Developed Countries*, St Martin's Press, New York.

Cornelius, A. (1987), 'Jaguar Leaps into the Designer Age', *Guardian*, 26 May.

Crockford, D. (1994), 'Strategic Management in Privatized Businesses', *Long Range Planning*, vol. 27, no. 2, pp. 111-18.

Cummings, L.L. (1984), 'Compensation, Culture and Motivation: A Systems Perspective', *Organisational Dynamics*, vol. 13, no. 4, pp. 33-44.

David, S.M. (1984), *Managing Corporate Culture*, Ballinger, Cambridge, Mass.

Davies, J. and Easterby-Smith, M. (1985), 'Organisational Myths from the Perspective of Evaluation', paper presented at the ATM Research in Management Conference, Ashridge, January.

Davis, S.M. and Schwartz, H. (1981), 'Matching Corporate Culture and Business Strategy', *Organisational Dynamics*, vol. 10, pp. 30-48, Summer.

Deal, T.E. and Kennedy, A.A. (1982), *Corporate Cultures: The Rites and Rituals of Corporate Lives,* Addison-Wesley, Reading, Mass.

Deer, C.B. (1986), *Managing the New Careerists*, Jossey-Bass, San Francisco.

Denison, D.R. (1990), *Corporate Culture and Organisational Effectiveness*, John Wiley & Sons, New York.

Denzin, N.K. (1989), *Interpretative Interactionism*, Sage, London.

Driver, M.J. and Coombs, M.W. (1983), 'The Fit Between Career Concepts, Corporate Culture, Engineering Productivity and Morale', paper presented at the IEEE Careers Conference.

Dumain, B. (1990), 'Creating a New Company Culture', *Fortune*, pp. 55-8, 15 January.

Dumphy, D. and Stace, D. (1993), 'The Strategic Management of Corporate Change', *Human Relations*, vol. 46, no. 8.

Durkheim, E. (1953), *Sociology and Philosophy*, Cohen and West, London.

Dyer, L. (1982), 'Culture in Organisations: A Case Study and Analysis', Sloan Management School, M.I.T. working paper.

Dyer, L. (1984), 'Studying Human Resources Strategy: An Approach and an Agenda', *Industrial Relations*, vol. 23, no. 2, pp. 156-69.

Dyer, W.G. (1980), *Culture Change in Family Firms: Anticipating and Managing Business and Family Transitions*, Jossey-Bass, San Francisco.

Easterby-Smith, M. (1988), 'Evaluating the Development of Corporate Cultures: A Case for Naturalist Methods?', *Management Education and Development*, vol. 19, no. 2, pp. 85-99.

Edwards, J.D. and Kleiner, B.H. (1988), 'Transforming Organisational Values and Culture Effectively', *Leadership and Organisational Development Journal*, vol. 9, no. 1, pp. 13-16.

Ellen, R.F. (1984), *Ethnographic Research*, Academic Press, London.

Feldman, D.C. (1988), *Managing Careers in Organisations*, Scott, Foresman and Co., New York.

Ferguson, P. (1992), 'Privatisation Options for Eastern Europe', *World Economy*, vol. 15, no. 4, pp. 487-504.

Filatotchev, I., Buck, T. and Wright, M. (1993), 'Privatization: The Sale of the Century', *The Appraisal Journal*, October.

Fishlock, D. (1986), 'Man with a Mission to Set the Record Straight on BNFL', *Financial Times*, 2 April.

Fitzgerald, T.H. (1988), 'Can Change in Organisational Culture Really be Managed?', *Organisational Dynamics*, vol. 17, pp. 5-15, Autumn.

Fombrum, C. (1982), 'Environmental Trends Create New Pressures on Human Resources', *Journal of Business Strategy*, vol. 3, no. 1, pp. 61-9.

Foster, G. (1988), 'Britain's Nervous', *Management Today*, pp. 48-54, April.

Fraser, R. (1986), *Privatization: The UK Experience*, Longman Group.

Freire, P. (1976), *Education: The Practice of Freedom*, Writers and Readers, London.

Freud, S. (1940), 'An Outline of Psychoanalysis', *International Journal of Psychoanalysis*, vol. 21, pp. 27-89.

Frost, J., Moore, L.F., Louis, M.R., Lundberg, C.C. and Martin, J. (1985), *Organisational Culture*, Sage, Beverly Hills.

Fulmer, F.M. and Gilkey, R. (1988), 'Blending Corporate Families: Management and Organisation Development in a Postmerger Environment', *Academy of Management Executive*, vol. II, no. 4, pp. 275-83.

Gabarro, J.J. (1985), 'When a Manager Takes Charge', *Harvard Business Review*, vol. 63, no. 3, pp. 110-23.

Gabel, L. (1987), 'Privatisation: Its Motives and Likely Consequences' INSEAD Working Paper, Fontainebleau, France.

Gaertner, K.N. (1988), 'Managers' Careers and Organisational Change', *Academy of Management Executive*, vol. II, no. 4, pp. 311-18.

Gelbtuch, H. (1993), 'Privatisation: The Sale of the Century', *Appraisal Journal*, pp. 478-82, October.

Glaser, B. and Strauss, A. (1967), *The Discovery of Grounded Theory*, Aldine, Chicago.

Gordon, G.G. (1985), 'The Relationship of Corporate Culture to Industry Sector and Corporate Performance', in Kilmann, R.H. et al (eds.), *Gaining Control of the Corporate Culture*, Jossey-Bass, San Francisco.

Green, S. (1988), 'Understanding Corporate Culture and its Relation to Strategy', *International Studies of Management and Organisations*, vol. XVIII, no. 2, pp. 6-28.

Griffiths, J. (1988), 'Egan Shifts Jaguar into Second Gear', *Financial Times*, 25 August.

Gross, W. and Schichman, S. (1987), 'How to Grow an Organisation Culture', *Personnel*, vol. 64, pp. 52-6, September.

Gunz, H. (1987), 'The Dual Meaning of Managerial Careers: Organisational and Individual Levels of Analysis', unpublished paper, Manchester Business School.

Gunz, H. (1989), *Careers and Corporate Cultures: Managerial Mobility in Large Corporations*, Basil Blackwell, Oxford.

Hall, D.T. and Hall, E.T. (1976), 'What is New in Career Management', *Organisational Dynamics*, vol. 5, pp. 17-33, Spring.

Hammer, R.M., Hinterhuber, H.H. and Lorentz, J. (1989), 'Privatization: A Cure for all Ills?', *Long Range Planning*, vol. 22, no. 6, pp. 19-28.

Handy, C.B. (1976), 'So You Want to Change your Organisation? Then First Identify its Culture', *Management Education and Development*, vol. 7, pp. 67-84.

Harrison, R. (1987), *Organisation Culture and Quality of Service: A Strategy for Releasing Love in the Work Place*, Association for Management Education and Development, London.

Helman, A. (1991), 'Kibbutz Systems, Efficiency and Privatization', Paper presented at The International Privatization Conference at the University of St. Andrews, Scotland.

Henry, E. and Moore, A. (1982), *Sociology*, Penguin, London.

Hick, H.G. and Gullet, C.R. (1981), *Multinational Management*, McGraw Hill, New York.

Hofstede, G. (1980), *Culture's Consequences: International Differences in Work Related Values*, Sage, Beverly Hills.

Hofstede, G. (1986), 'The Usefulness of the Organisational Culture Concept', *Journal of Management Studies*, vol. 23, no. 3, pp. 20-25.

Hofstede, G., Newjen, B., Ohayv, D.D. and Sanders, G. (1990), 'Measuring Organisational Cultures: A Qualitative and Quantitative Study Across Twenty Cases', *Administrative Science Quarterly*, vol. 35, no. 2, pp. 286-316.

Huseman, R.C., Alexander III, and Driver, R.W. (1980), 'Planning for Organisational Change: The Role of Communication', *Managerial Planning*, vol. 28, no. 6, pp. 32-6.

Ivancevich, J.M. and Donnelly, J.H. (1975), 'Relation of Organisational Structure to Job Satisfaction, Anxiety-Stress and Performance', *Administrative Science Quarterly*, vol. 20, pp. 272-80.

Jaques, E. (1951), *The Changing Culture of a Factory*, Routledge & Kegan Paul, London.

Jelinek, M., Smircich, L. and Hirsch, P. (1983), 'Introduction: A Code of Many Colours', *Administrative Science Quarterly*, vol. 28, no. 2, pp. 331-8.

Kateb, G. (1966), 'Utopia and the Good Life,' in Manual, F.E. (ed.), *Utopias and Utopian Thought*, A Condor Book, Souvenir Press.

Keat, R. (1991), *Enterprise Culture*, Routledge, London.

Keat, R. and Abercrombie, N. (eds.) (1991), *Enterprise Culture*, Routledge.

Kerr, J. (1987), 'Corporate Culture and Reward Systems', *Academy of Management Executive*, pp. 99-107, May.

Kerr, J. and Slocum, J.W. (1987), 'Managing Corporate Culture Through Reward Systems', *Academy of Management Executive*, vol. 1, no. 2, pp. 99-107.

Kilmann, R.M., Saxton, M.J. and Serpa, R. (1985), *Gaining Control of the Corporate Culture*, Jossey-Bass, San Francisco.

Kilmann, R.M., Saxton, M.J. and Serpa, R. (1986), 'Issues in Understanding and Changing Culture', *California Management Review*, vol. XXVIII, no. 2, pp. 87-94.

King, L. (1989), 'Profits Hit a Record - But Costs Up Too', *British Airways' News*, p.1, 26 May.

Kirsch, M.P. (1988), 'Organisational Culture adds a Third Control System: A Cognitive Approach', unpublished Doctoral Dissertation, Michigan State University.

Kroeber, A.L. and Kluckhohn, C. (1952), *Culture*, Massachusetts Museum.

Kroeber, A.L. and Parsons, T. (1958), 'The Concepts of Culture and Social System', *American Sociological Review*, vol. 23, no. 4, pp. 582-3.

Laraia, R.B. (1986), *Cultura*, Zahar, Rio de Janeiro.

Lee, R.A. (1985), 'Researching Managerial Promotion', *Management Research News*, vol. 8, no. 4, pp. 23-31.

Lee, R.A. and Piper, J. (1988), 'Dimensions of Promotion Culture in Midland Bank', *Personnel Review*, vol. 17, no. 6, pp. 15-24.

Linkow, P. (1989), 'Is Your Culture Ready for Total Quality?', *Quality Progress*, vol. 22, no. 11, pp. 69-71.

Lorsch, J.W. (1986), 'Managing Culture: The Invisible Barrier to Strategic Change', *California Management Review*, vol. XXVIII, no. 2, pp. 95-109.

MacMillan, I.C. and Schuler, R.S. (1985), 'Gaining a Competitive Edge Through Human Resources', *Personnel*, vol. 62, no. 4, pp. 24-9.

McClelland, D.C. (1961), *The Achieving Society*, Van Nostrand Co., Princeton.

McIntosh, C. (1994), 'To Market to Market', *Futurist*, vol. 28, no. 1, pp. 24-8.

Macrae, N. (1992), 'Future Privatizations', *The Economist*, 3 January.

Marglin, S.A. (1994), 'Losing touch: the Cultural Conditions of Worker Accommodation and Resistance' in Marglin, F.A. and Marglin, S.A. (eds.), *Dominating Knowledge*, pp 217-82, Clarendon Press, Oxford.

Martin J. and Meyerson, D. (1988), 'Organisational Cultures and the Denial, Channelling and Acknowledgement of Ambiguity in Managing Ambiguity and Change', in Pondy, L.R. et al (eds.), *Managing Ambiguity and Change*, John Wiley and Sons, New York.

Mason, J. (1991), 'Europe's Privatization Party', *International Management*, pp. 30-3, December.

Mattsson, J. (1985), 'Developing an Axiological Method to Measure Company Values', *European Journal of Marketing*, vol. 22, no. 6, pp. 21-34.

Meares, L.B. (1986), 'A Model for Changing Organisational Culture', *Personnel*, vol. 63, pp. 38-42, July.

Meyerson, D. and Martin J. (1987), 'Cultural Change: An Integration of Different Views', *Journal of Management Studies*, vol. 24, no. 6, pp. 623-47.

Miles, M.B. (1979), 'Qualitative Data as an Attractive Nuisance: The Problem of Analysis', *Administrative Science Quarterly*, vol. 24, pp. 590-601, December.

Miles, M.B. and Huberman, A.M. (1984), *Qualitative Data Analysis: A Sourcebook of New Methods*, Sage, Beverly Hills.

Miller, A.N. (1994), 'Privatization: Lessons from the British Experience', *Long Range Planning*, vol. 27, no. 6, pp. 125-36.

Mintzberg, H. (1979), 'An Emerging Strategy of "Direct" Research', in Maanen, J.V. (ed.), *Qualitative Methodology*, Sage, Beverly Hills.

Montagu-Pollock, M. (1990), 'Privatization: What Went Wrong?', *Asian Business Review*, vol. 26, pp. 32-9.

Morgan, G. (1986), *Images of Organisation*, Sage, London.

Morgan, G. (1988), *Riding the Waves of Change: Developing Managerial Competencies for a Turbulent World*, Jossey-Bass, London.

Morgan, G. and Smircich, L. (1980), 'The Case for Qualitative Research', *Academy of Management Review*, vol. 5, no. 4, pp. 491-500.

Morgan, M.A., Hall, T. and Martier, A. (1980), 'Career Development Strategies in Industry: Where Are We and Where Should We Be?', in Morgan, M. (ed.), *Managing Career Development*, Litton, New York.

Muti D.M. (1990), 'Privatization of Socialist Economics: General Issues and the Polish Case', OECD conference on 'The Transformation of Poland Economics', Paris (20-22 June).

Neto, E.S. (1991), 'Brazilian Privatisation: Liability Regime for Participants', *International Financial Law Review*, vol. 10, no. 5, pp. 36-8.

Ogbonna, E. and Wilkinson, B., (1990), 'Corporate Strategy and Corporate Culture: The View from the Check-out', *Personnel Review*, vol. 19 (4), p. 333.

O'Toole, J.J. (1979), 'Corporate and Managerial Cultures', in Cooper, C.L. (ed.), *Behavioural Problems in Organisations*, Prentice-Hall, Englewood Cliffs, N.J.

Parker, D. (1995), 'Privatization and Agency Status: Identifying the Critical Factors for Performance Improvement', *British Journal of Management*, vol. 6, pp. 29-43.

Pascale, R. and Athos, A.G. (1981), *The Art of Japanese Management: Applications for American Executives*, Simon and Schuster, New York.

Pascale, R. (1985), 'The Paradox of Corporate Culture: Reconciling Ourselves to Socialisation', *California Management Review*, vol. XXVII, no. 2, pp. 26-41.

Payne, R. (1991), 'Taking Stock of Corporate Culture', *Personnel Management*, pp. 26-9, July.

Peters, T.J. and Waterman, R.H. (1982), *In Search of Excellence*, Harper and Row, New York.

Pettigrew, A.M. (1979), 'On Studying Organisational Cultures', *Administrative Science Quarterly*, vol. 24, pp. 570-81, December.

Pettigrew, A.M. (1985), *The Awakening Giant: Continuity and Change in Imperial Chemical Industries*, Basil Blackwell, Oxford.

Pettigrew, A.M. (1987), *The Management of Strategic Change*, Basil Blackwell, London.

Pettigrew, A.M. (1988), 'Longitudinal Field Research on Change: Theory and Practice', paper presented at the National Science Foundation Conference on Longitudinal Research Methods in Organisations, Austin, Texas, September.

Piercy and Peattie, (1988), 'Matching Marketing Strategies to Corporate Culture', *Journal of General Manager*, vol. 3/4, pp. 33-44.

Porter, L. and Lawler, E. (1965), 'Properties of Organisation Structure in Relation to Job Attitudes and Job Behaviour', *Psychological Bulletin*, vol. 64, no. 1, pp. 23-51.

Porter, P. (1988), *Jaguar*, Sidgwick and Jackson, London.

Ramanadahan, V.V. (ed.), (1988), *Privatisation in the UK*, Routledge, London.

Rhodes, W.R. (1992), 'A New Perspective on Latin America', *World of Banking*, vol. 11, no. 4, pp. 25-8, 33.

Rokeach, M. (1973), *The Nature of Human Values*, Free Press, New York.

Salama, A. (1991), 'Privatisation and Culture Change: Four Case Studies of UK Large Organisations', paper presented at the International Conference on Privatization at St Andrews University, September.

Salama, A. (1992), 'Privatisacao e Mundanca Cultural: Uma Experiencia Brazileira, Usiminas', Revista de Admistracao Publica 1992, FGV, Rio de Janeiro, Autumn.

Salama, A. (1992), 'The Use of an Organisation's Biography as a Research Method for Investigating Organisational Development', *Management Education and Development*, vol. 23, part 3, pp. 225-33.

Salama, A. and Easterby-Smith, M. (1994), 'Cultural Change on Managerial Careers', *Personnel Review*, vol. 23, no. 3.

Sathe, V. (1985), *Culture and Related Corporate Realities*, Irwin, Homewood, Illinois.

Savona, D. (1993), 'Cast off the State', *International Business*, pp. 64-70, October.

Schein, E.H. (1971), 'The Individual, The Organisation and The Career: A Conceptual Scheme', *Journal of Applied Behavioural Science*, vol. 7, no. 4, pp. 401-25.

Schein, E.H. (1977), 'Career Development', in Hackman, R.J. and Subtle, J.L. (eds.), *Improving Life at Work*, Goodyear, Santa Monica.

Schein, E.H. (1978), *Career Dynamics: Matching Individual and Organisational Needs*, Addison-Wesley, Reading, Mass.

Schein, E.H. (1983a), 'The Role of the Founder in Creating Organisational Cultures', *Organisational Dynamics*, vol. 12, pp. 13-29, Summer.

Schein, E.H. (1983b), 'Corporate Culture: What it is and How to Change it?', Sloan School of Management (MIT), Working Paper, ONR TR-26-no.v.

Schein, E.H. (1984a), 'The Role of the Founder in Creating Organizational Cultures', *Organizational Dynamics*, vol. 12, pp. 13-28, Summer.

Schein, E.H. (1984b), 'Coming to a New Awareness of Organisational Culture', *Sloan Management Review*, vol. 25, pp. 3-15, Winter.

Schein, E.H. (1984c), 'Culture as an Environmental Context for Careers', *Journal of Occupational Behaviour*, vol. 5, no. 1, pp. 71-81.

Schein, E.H. (1985a), *Organisational Culture and Leadership*, Jossey-Bass, San Francisco.

Schein, E.H. (1985b), 'How Cultures Form, Develop and Change', in Kilmann, R.H. et al (eds.), *Gaining Control of the Corporate Culture*, Jossey-Bass, London.

Schein, E.H. (1985c), 'A Critical Look at Current Career Development Theory and Research', in Hall, D.T. (ed.), *Career Development in Organisations*, Jossey-Bass, San Francisco.

Schein, E.H. (1986), 'Are you Corporate Cultured?', *Personnel Journal*, vol. 15, no. v, pp. 83-96.

Schein, E.H. (1986), *Organizational Culture and Leadership*, Jossey-Bass, San Francisco.

Schein, E.H. (1987), *The Clinical Perspective in Fieldwork*, Sage, Beverly Hills.

Scherreik, S. (1994), 'Your Ticket to the Privatization Party', *Business Week*, p. 134, 19 April.

Schneider, S.C. (1988), 'National vs Corporate Culture: Implications for Human Resources Management', *Human Resources Management*, vol. 27, no. 2, pp. 231-46.

Schuler, R.S. and Jackson, S.E. (1987), 'Linking Competitive Strategies with Human Resources Management Practices', *Academy of Management Executive*, vol. 1, no. 3, pp. 207-19.

Schuler, R.S. and Jackson, S.E. (1987), 'Organisational Strategy and Organisational Level as Determinants of Human Resource Management Practices', *Human Resource Planning*, 10 (3), pp. 125-41.

Schultz, A. (1970), *On Phenomenology and Social Relations*, University of Chicago Press, Chicago.

Schwartz, H. and David, S.M. (1981), 'Matching Corporate Culture and Business Strategy', *Organizational Dynamics*, vol. 10, pp. 30-47, Summer.

Sears, A. (1992), 'The Action in Latin America', *Global Finance*, vol. 6, no. 3, p. 112.

Sethia, N.K. and Glinow, M.A. (1986), 'Arriving at Four Cultures by Managing the Reward System', in Kilmann, R.H. et al (eds.), *Gaining Control of the Corporate Culture*, Jossey-Bass, San Francisco.

Silverman, D. (1985), *Qualitative Methodology*, Gower Press, London.

Skinner, W. (1986), 'The Productivity Paradox', *Harvard Business Review*, vol. 64, no. 4, pp. 55-9.

Smircich, L. (1983), 'Concepts of Culture and Organisational Analysis', *Administrative Science Quarterly*: vol. 28, pp. 339-58.

Smith, A. (1776), *An Inquiry into the Nature and Causes of the Wealth of Nations*, W. Strahan and T. Cadell, London.

Smith, A.M. and Lewis, B.R. (1989), 'Customer Care in Financial Service Organisations', *International Journal of Bank Marketing*, vol. 7, no. 5, pp. 13-22.

Smith, P.E., Barnard, J. M. and Smith G. (1986), 'Privatization and Cultural Change ' *Journal of Management Development*, vol. 5, no. 2, pp. 51-61.

Stumpf, S.A. and London, M. (1981), 'Management Promotions: Individual Factors Influencing the Decision Process', *Academy of Management Review*, vol. 6, no. 4, pp. 539-49.

Swierczek, F.W., (1992), 'Management of Change in Telecommunications: A Cultural Approach', *Strategic Management of Information and Telecommunications Technology*, vol. 7, nos. 6/7/8, pp. 409-23.

Syrett, M. (1988), 'Managers Have Skills, But Just What Are They?', *Sunday Times*, 6 March.

Thackray, J. (1986), 'The Corporate Culture Rage', *Management Today*, pp. 67-9, February.

Thomas, A. (1981), 'The Career Graph: A Tool for Mid-Career Development', *Personnel Review*, vol. 10, no. 3, pp. 18-22.

Tichy, N. (1982), 'The Essentials of Strategic Change Management', *Journal of Business Strategy*, vol. 3, no. 4, pp. 55-67.

Townsend, R. (1971), *Up the Organisation*, Knopf, New York.

Trice, H.M. and Beyer, J.M. (1984), 'Studying Organisational Cultures Through Rites and Ceremonials', *Academy of Management Review*, vol. 9, no. 4, pp. 653-69.

Tunstall, W.B. (1983), 'Cultural Transition at AT&T', *Sloan Management Review*, vol. 24, pp. 15-26, Fall.

Turner, R. (1991), 'More Trouble in Brazil', *Global Finance*, vol. 5, no. 9, p. 33.

Tylor, E.B. (1924), *Primitive Culture*, Smith, Gloucester, Mass. (first published in 1871).

Utt, R.D. (1989), 'Privatization: Shifting the Balance towards Growth', *Economic Impact*, no. 69, April.

Van Mannen, J. (ed.) (1983), *Qualitative Methodology*, Sage, Beverly Hills.

Wagner, H.R. (1975), *Alfred Scutz: on Phenomenology and Social Relations*, Chicago University Press, Chicago.

Walters, P. (1990), *Privatisation, Implications for Cultural Change*, United Research, London.

Watson, T. (1963), *A Business and its Beliefs: The Ideas that Helped Build IBM*, McGraw-Hill, New York.

Wilkins, A.L. and Patterson, K.J. (1985), 'You Can't Get There from Here: What Will Make Culture-Change Projects Fail?', in Kilmann, R.H. et al (eds.), *Gaining Control of the Corporate Culture*, Jossey-Bass, San Francisco.

Woodward, N. (1988), 'Managing Cultural Change in Privatisation', in Romanadham, V.V. (ed.), *Privatisation in the UK*, Routledge, London.

Woodward, N. (1989), 'From Nationalisation to Privatisation - the UK Experience', in Halsi, T., *Strategic Issues in State Controlled Organisations*, JAI Press, Greenwich.

Yarrow, G.K. (1986), 'Privatization in Theory and Practice', *Economic Policy*, no. 2, pp. 324-77.

Yarrow, G. (1988), 'Privatization and Economic Performance', *The Economic Review*, p. 205, November.

Yin, R.K. (1981a), 'The Case Study Crisis: Some Answers', *Administrative Science Quarterly*, vol. 26, no. 1, pp. 58-65.

Yin, R.K. (1981b), 'The Case Study as a Serious Research Strategy', *Knowledge: Creation, Diffusion and Utilisation*, vol. 3, no. 1, pp. 97-114.

Young, D. (1989), 'Putting the Customer First', unpublished paper, David Young Consultancy Services.